Bluegrass Mandolin
for the Complete Ignoramus!
by
Wayne Erbsen

Order Number: NGB-107

ISBN 978-1-883206-55-0

Come visit us at www.nativeground.com

IOU

Writing this book is a lot like standing on stage playing mandolin in a bluegrass band. Without the band, it's mighty lonesome up there. Thanks to my "band" for all their backup and support: Kelli Churchill for transcribing the music, Steve Millard for cover art, Martin Fox, Wes Erbsen and Arlin Geyer for photography, Jamie Hooper for editing photographs, Dave Freeman and Neil Rosenberg for historical information on "Paul and Silas," Barbara Swell, Janet Swell, John Miller, Ralph Julian, Marie Gantz, Hilary Dirlam, Rita Miller and Mark Wingate for proofreading and editing. Thanks also to Dave freeman for permission to use "I've Just Seen the Rock of Ages."

Photo by Martin Fox

Bill Monroe, Jack Hicks, Joe Stuart and Monroe Fields

Instructional Audio

An essential part of this book is the audio, which you can find online at **www.nativeground.com/audio** to download or stream. You will also find the lyrics to all 28 songs! I recorded a whopping 92 cuts so you can hear all the tunes, the scales and even the variations on the tunes. Throughout the book you'll find illustrations of an old gramophone with numbers inside it. These numbers correspond to the audio track numbers. The mandolin is balanced to the right speaker and rhythm guitar is on the left. You can monkey with the balance knob if you want to have more mandolin and less guitar, or vice versa. It wouldn't hurt my feelings if you turned the mandolin completely off and just used the guitar track to back up your mandolin pickin'. If you need an old-fashioned CD please give us a call at 800-752-2656 or email info@nativeground.com.

Contents

Contents

Photo by Martin Fox

Parts of a Mandolin(ist)

Cowlick

Adam's Apple

Nut

Peghead

Tuners

Tailpiece

Bridge

F Hole

Stump

Come in the Door!

In my home state of North Carolina, I often say, "Come in the door!" when I'm welcoming someone into our home. You just never know when someone might come in through the window. So come in the door, and have a seat right over there. Your mandolin? Yes. Go ahead and get it out, because you can't play it in the case.

Before I teach you to play the mandolin, let me explain why I wrote this book for the so-called "Ignoramus." The title is nothing more than a not-so-clever marketing ploy designed to get you in the door. It worked! I'm guessing that you're a playful person who wants to learn the mandolin, but is intimidated by more formal teaching materials. As you've already noticed, I use a sometimes silly and casual approach. That's because if you're like me, you HATE being bored and you'd rather laugh than cry. I figure if you're laughing, you're having fun and if you also learn to play the mandolin, hey, that's a bonus!

Let me put you at ease by saying that I've spent the last 45 years figuring out how to make learning to play a musical instrument EASY. In fact, around Asheville, North Carolina, people whisper that, "Wayne Erbsen can even teach a FROG to play music." I started writing instruction books for beginners way back in 1973 when I published my first book, *How to play the Banjo for the Complete Ignoramus!* Since then, I've done over two dozen instruction books and songbooks that have taught folks just like you to play.

Photo by Wayne Erbsen

Let's be clear about one thing. **THIS BOOK IS FOR THE TOTAL AND ABSOLUTE BEGINNER.** 'Course, if you're only a quasi or semi-beginner, we'll let you in the door too. To squeeze the most out of this book, you DON'T have to know how to read music, be able to tap your foot, know your chords or be kin to Bill Monroe. All you need is the itch to learn to play your mandolin. The rest will be easy. Trust me.

Do You Have the GUTS to be an Ignoramus?

I can count on forty fingers the times someone has looked at one of my books for the Ignoramus, and said, "THAT'S ME." If you picked up this book when you saw the title and said, "That's me," this IS the book for you. If you're wondering whether you have the smarts to be an ignoramus, let me assure you. THIS IS AS SIMPLE AS A MANDOLIN BOOK GETS. You are in the right place. Now, Turn the page.

Bluegrass Mandolin

So what is "bluegrass mandolin?" The answer has only one word: "Bill." That's the legendary Bill Monroe, of course. He pretty much invented a style that we now call "bluegrass mandolin." Before Bill came along, the mandolin was a delicate sounding instrument that was more often played in the parlor than at a barn dance. In Bill's hands, the mandolin was no longer the timid instrument that played popular and classical printed music sitting daintily on a music stand. Instead, he single-handedly turned the mandolin into a passionate and powerful instrument that could evoke a wide range of deeply-felt emotions. So are you going to sound like Bill by the time you finish reading this book? Gosh no! That would take at least two books. What we ARE going to do is simplify bluegrass mandolin down to the basic ingredients and make it easy for you.

Bill Monroe

So what are the basic ingredients of bluegrass mandolin? Nothing more than melody and rhythm. That's it! Once you get past all the fluff, the melody of most bluegrass songs is pretty dang simple and straightforward. If you can play one melody, you can play practically any of them. And the rhythm? It can be as simple as ONE, ONE, ONE ONE, or as complicated as a Latin drummer caught in a tornado. We'll start with the simple approach, OK?

Before we jump into the pond, let's first just stick our toe in the water and be clear about what we're going to learn. 1) The bare-bones melody of 28 songs, 2) simplified chords to play back-up to these songs, 3) harmony chords to enhance the melody and 4) several simple rhythms to pep up the basic melody. As we mix up or alternate some of these rhythms, you'll discover the magic of improvising.

PLAYING BY EAR. As much as I hate to admit it, this book is POISON. I say that because many of you will learn these melodies note for note and become addicted to reading off a sheet of paper. I dread being responsible for that! What I really want you to do is learn these songs so well that you can close the book and still be able to play the tunes in your own way. I want you to be able to improvise and to be able to play by ear. How do you play by ear? 1) Learn your scales really well by heart and be able to play them backwards and forwards. 2) Using the scales, try picking out little melodies that you are very familiar with, be it "Jingle Bells," or "Happy Birthday to You." You should try playing any melody that you can sing or hum. 3) Use the CD that comes with this book to your advantage. Pick out a song you're familiar with on the CD and play it over and over. Try to find some of the notes without looking at the book. Can't do it? Then look at just the first few notes in the book and then close the book and try it by ear. With practice and determination you'll soon get the hang of playing by ear. Stick with it!

Important Stuff!

If this book doesn't get you started playing the mandolin, I'll eat my hat. Before you ask me to start chewing, be sure to read the vital information on this page. In the meantime, excuse me while I put on my bib.

First, note that your book comes fully equipped with a CD where I play all the scales and the twenty-eight tunes that are found in this book at a moderately slow tempo. All through the book you'll see an illustration of an old gramophone with numbers inside. The numbers tell you the track numbers on the CD that correspond to the music in the book. NOTE: If you open the CD with your computer, you'll find Word files with the complete lyrics to all the songs.

The book is arranged so that on the following pages you'll find vital information on tuning, how to hold your mandolin and how to hold the pick. Then I'll carefully explain how to read tab or tablature and you'll see how easy it is to play the G scale. Even easier will be your first tune, "Joy to the World."

Each song in the book is laid out on two facing pages. At the top of the left hand page, you'll find a short history of the song. This will come in handy when you're intro-ducing the song on stage. (I'm not joking!) At the top right hand side of this page is a chart showing you where to find the notes for this song (see left). You'll then be shown how to play the simple melody (ICE COLD LICKS), a slightly more advanced arrangement (WARM LICKS), and for those brave souls, HOT LICKS. At the bottom of the page you'll find a box with tips on playing harmony notes.

```
       Index              Ring
A ——————B——————————————————————
D —————————E———————————————G————
```

On the right hand page is the tab and music of the song, complete with the chords, and as many of the lyrics as can fit on the page. Just to the left of the title at the top of this page is the key the song is in. What is a key? A key gives you such vital informa-tion as what scale and chords are used in the song. As we progress through the book, we'll learn songs in the keys of G, A, F, C and D. Keep in mind that the songs in each key are arranged alphabetically to make them easy to find. You'll soon notice that there are many more tunes in the key of G than any other key. Why? When you start jamming with other beginning bluegrassers, you'll see that G is their favorite key. So when the day comes when you unfurl your mandolin to start jamming in the popular key of G, you'll be loaded for bear.

> As you play through the tunes in the book, you'll soon realize that most of the tunes are simplified down to the bare-bones melody. The nonessential notes have been left out, and all that remains is the skeleton of the tune. In order to read the tablature or music, it is vital that you memorize the names of the open strings of the mandolin as well as all the notes of the scale you are fixing to play.

Tuning Your Mandolin

Job one will be getting your mandolin in tune. Good luck! If you've never tuned a stringed instrument before, you might need help. Ask a friend who plays mandolin or guitar to give you a hand tuning it. You can always throw yourself on the mercy of your local music store; they will surely take pity on you. If no help can be found, fine. You can tune it yourself.

ELECTRONIC TUNER: I highly recommend you purchase an electronic tuner to help you get in tune. These little gadgets are easily available at your local music store. Be sure to bring your mandolin with you when you purchase a tuner and get the salesperson to show you how it works.

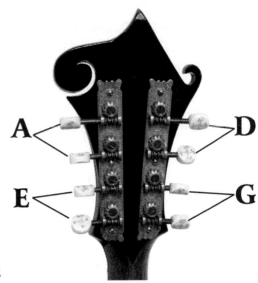

Photo by Martin Fox

Heck, why don't you get him or her to go ahead and tune your mandolin for you so you can start out on the right foot. You can reward them by being a loyal customer.

The Strings of the Mandolin

1st = E, 2nd =A, 3rd = D, 4th = G

USING YOUR ELECTRONIC TUNER: Although electronic tuners vary from one brand to another, they all basically do the same thing: tell you the name of the note you're playing, and whether it's too high or too low. Check out the names of the strings in the box above. You'll need to memorize the names of your strings, and the sooner the better. To help you memorize them, you can make up your own acronym or use this one: "Elephants Always Do Go." Remember that the 1st string is the string that's closest to the floor, when you are holding your mandolin in playing position.

TUNING TIPS: When you're tuning your mandolin, I suggest starting with the E strings, and then go on to the A, D and G. With your mandolin on your lap, you will turn the E and A string pegs clockwise to make the string go up, or sharp, in musician's lingo. On the G and D strings, turning the peg counterclockwise will make the string go sharp. With your pick try to play and tune only one string at a time, no small trick.

Tuning Your Mandolin

Your mandolin comes fully equipped with four pairs of strings. Each pair should be tuned exactly the same.

TURNING YOUR TUNING PEGS. This tuning tip is so important, I think I'll just put it in a box so you can't possibly miss it.

> When you're tuning a string, play the string continually as you are turning the peg.

NO ELECTRONIC TUNER? Let's say you're an old-fashioned person who doesn't cotton to newfangled 'lectric gizmos. Great! I admire that. In that case, you can tune the mandolin to practically any other musical instrument.

Charlie Bowman & Tony Alderman

GUITAR: If you can find a tuned guitar, you can compare the notes of the mandolin with those of the guitar. The 1st string of the guitar is an E and the 1st or E string of your mandolin should match that. If you fret the guitar's third string at the second fret, you'll get an A. You can change your A string to sound like that. Next, fret the second string of the guitar at the third fret and make your D string sound like that. Finally, play the guitar's third string open (unfretted) and match your G string to that. That's it!

FIDDLE: It's a snap to tune your mandolin to a fiddle because they're both tuned the same.

TUNING BY THE FRET METHOD: With this method, you can tune the mandolin to itself. Begin by getting the two E strings in tune to each other. You're then going to tune your A string by fretting the A string at the 7th fret and making it sound like the E string played open. After you get both A strings adjusted, you'll be tuning the D string to the A string. You can do this by fretting the D string at the 7th fret and making it sound like the A string played open. Finally, fret the G string at the 7th fret and make it sound like the D string played open.

PITCH PIPES: Used to be, pitch pipes were one of the few tools folks had to tune their instruments. Any more, they're rarely used because they're not terribly accurate. If you have an old pitchpipe similar to the one in this drawing, hold on to it. It's an antique and you can pass it on to your grandkids as a relic of your misspent youth.

NOTE: Mandolins are somewhat finicky and are hard to get exactly in tune. The double strings seem to play tricks on your ears. If you can't get it quite right, you're in good company, as there are many thousands of other out-of-tune mandolins being played at this very moment.

How to Hold the Mandolin

My, my, my, how things have changed! In the waning days of the 19th century, this would have been you in this photo, unless, of course, you're a member of the opposite sex. If you could see the back of his instrument, you would notice that it has a bowl-shaped back, which is next to impossible to hold steady. That's why he's got it cradled in a nest between his arm and chest.

Although these ornate instruments were a joy to look at and sounded sweet, holding them was like trying to dance with a wet seal. They slipped away from you.

Fortunately, in the early Twenties, master luthier Lloyd Loar of the Gibson Company started producing flat backed mandolins which are a dream to hold in comparison to the bowl backs, which we now call "tater bugs."

So how are you supposed to hold one? I definitely recommend using a strap. Although you can certainly attach it to the headstock of your mandolin, you'll find attaching it there will get in your way. Instead, I suggest you visit your trusted music store and have the repairman install a strap button on the underside of the neck nearest the body of the mandolin (see below). Using a strap will help you hold your mandolin steady while you pick it. It will also free up your hands so you don't have to support the neck of the mandolin to keep control of it.

Your left hand position is really important. Notice in the photo that my wrist is bent, my thumb is in the middle of the back of the neck, and there's a space between my hand and the bottom of the neck. The mandolin should be held in position either by a strap or by the pressure of your forearm pushing against the top of the mandolin near the tailpiece. Don't get into the habit of supporting the neck of the mandolin with your hand.

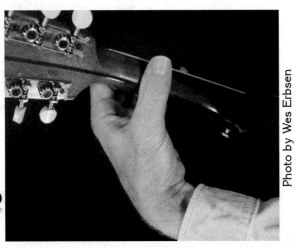

Photo by Wes Erbsen

FRETTING: The fingers of your left hand will push down on individual strings, an activity called "fretting." Be sure to use the very tips of your fingers and play in the space BETWEEN the little metal bars, called "frets." Never touch the metal fret itself. Your fingers need to push down hard enough on a string so the note rings clear. Push with your thumb on the back of the neck to get the strength you'll need to push the string down.

How to Hold the Pick

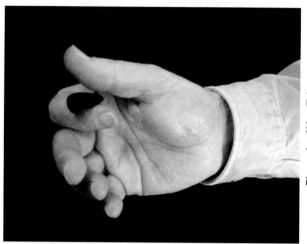

Photo by Wes Erbsen

The way you grip your pick will have a lot to do with your overall tone and how well you can maneuver over the strings. Begin by balancing your pick directly over the first joint of your index finger. Notice in the photo the direction the tip of the pick is pointing. Once you have the pick balanced like I do, secure it in place with your thumb. Be sure to keep your other fingers OPEN, so they sort of flap loosely as you play.

Most untrained beginners will naturally hold the pick with the very end of the index finger and the tip of the thumb. This might be good for dainty picking in the serenity of your living room. However, I am grooming you to project POWER and AUTHORITY with your mandolin, so the dainty pick hold certainly won't cut it. Remember, when you're finally released from Mandolin Boot Camp, you'll be playing with very loud bluegrass banjos and jumbo-sized guitars, and you're going to have to lay the power to it, and not let them kick sand in your face.

NOTE: As you pick individual notes, you will want to anchor your pinky finger loosely on the top of the mandolin to steady your hand. Keep your wrist relaxed and loose.

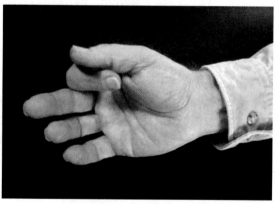

Photo by Wes Erbsen

Photo by Wes Erbsen

As you're picking, remember to keep your middle, ring, and pinky fingers OPEN, as in these photos. Be sure to play BOTH strings of the pair with your pick.

What kind of pick should you use? I recommend a teardrop-shaped pick, but beyond that, it all boils down to personal preference. I would stay away from the super thin and flexible pick, which is like hitting a fast ball with a boiled noodle.

Tablature or "Tab" for Ignoramuses

If you are a true and total beginner who doesn't read music, I have good news: all the tunes in the book are written out in an easy-to-read tab system that I invented. A line of tab will be right above a corresponding line of music, so if you sorta read music, you can look at both the tab and the music.

Take a look over at page 13 and almost half way down you'll see an example of the tab. It consists of four horizontal lines which represent the four pairs of strings on the mandolin. The E, or highest string, is found toward the top of the page and the G, or lowest string, is toward the bottom of the page. You'll notice that each string is marked on the left with its name. A letter on the string tells you the name of the note to play on that string.

TIMING: The timing in the tab matches the timing of the music. If you don't read music, no problem! Here's all you need to know. Each line of tab is divided into measures, which are the spaces between the "fence posts." At the beginning of the first line of music it will say 2/4, 3/4 or 4/4. The number on top tells you that each measure will either get two, three or four beats. Each beat is one tap of your foot (down and up). In the example below, look at the first line of the Carter Family song, "Keep on the Sunny Side of Life." The first two notes are both eighth notes. Your foot would go DOWN on the first eighth note and UP on the second. Then you'll see two notes with a single vertical line attached to it. Those are quarter notes and they each get one beat. For each quarter note, your foot would go DOWN-UP. In measure two, there are two pairs of eighth notes, so your foot would go DOWN or UP on each note. In measure 3, you'll see a D note with two lines attached. The two lines tell you it's a half note and gets two beats. This D note connects with a tie to a D note in measure 4, so the D note would get a total of three beats, or three DOWN-UPS with your foot.

Above the tab is a "G" and a "C" which are your chords. Take a look at page 15, to find vital information on playing the chords. On page 78 are simple rhythmic chord positions to play while you are singing and strumming the rhythm.

The Key of G

The G scale will be your new best friend. Start the scale with the G note on the D string with your ring finger. (D string at the 5th fret).

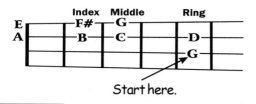

Start here.

The G Scale
G, A, B, C, D, E, F#, G

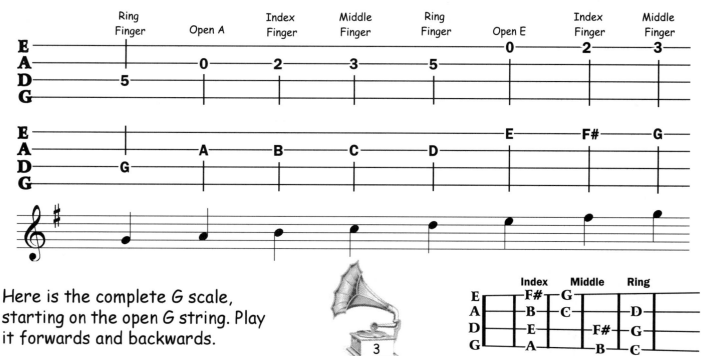

Here is the complete G scale, starting on the open G string. Play it forwards and backwards.

NOTE: Attached to each note in lines one and two, above, is a vertical line that tells you that each of these notes is a quarter note that gets one beat. It makes no difference if the line is attached to the top of the note (as in the G on the far left) or hanging down from the note (as in the G on the far right.)

Your First Tune!

et's put your G scale to work. Begin by playing the G scale (near the top of page 13) BACKWARDS, starting with your ring finger on the G note that you'll find on the fifth fret of the D string. Play it over and over until you can play the scale backwards without looking at the book. Now, you'll play these same notes, but this time change the timing to sound like the first line of "Joy to the World." Since you already know the tune, don't even look at the confusing tab or music below. Just play the first line of "Joy to the World" so it sounds right to your ears. When you can do that, play it starting on the E string at the third fret and again, play the scale backwards. When you get it sounding right, play it for a family member or friend and see if they can tell the name of the tune you're playing. If they can, you have arrived. If not, keep practicing!

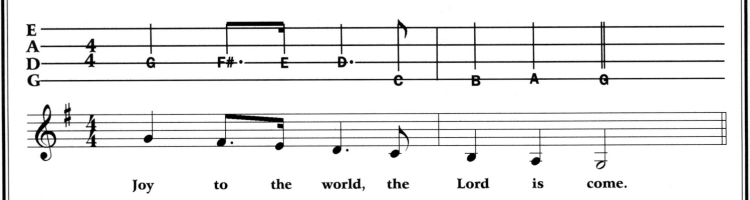

Joy   to   the   world,   the   Lord   is   come.

 Order of the Tunes to Play

For your convenience, the tunes in the book are arranged alphabetically within each key (G, A, F, C and D). The tunes that are the easiest to play tend to be the ones you've heard before, so feel free to play them in any order that works for you. Having said that, let me add that if you're a true Ignoramus, I would strongly point you toward these tunes to start with: "Down the Road," "Amazing Grace," "Shady Grove," "In the Pines," and "Cripple Creek."

Molasses Making in North Carolina

Photo by Wayne Erbsen

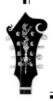

Mandolin Chords

Each song in the book includes chords that are written above the tab/music. For example, on page 19, you'll see a "G" near the beginning of line one of "Angel Band." What is a "chord?" It's nothing more than several notes are played at the same time and sound good, or harmonize, with each other. When you just want to accompany a song, you can simply play the chords. You can find the most common chord positions on page 78. When you're learning the chords, be sure to make your fingers go to the chords ALL AT THE SAME TIME. To practice this, go to a chord, then pick up your fingers about 1/4 of an inch, and set them back down totally at the same time. Practice, practice. Get into the habit of making your chords all at the same time right away. If you procrastinate on this, this bad habit will come back and bite you later. OUCH!

THE CHOP: Mandolin players have a unique way of playing chords, which is called the chop. The chop merely consists of striking down with a single brisk whack on the strings. The trick is knowing WHEN to chop.

one TWO

The Monroe Brothers

Tap your foot while saying "one" on the DOWN and "TWO" on the UP. Say the "TWO" a little louder than the "one." When you get this down cold, tap your foot, but this time only say the "TWO." Now go dig through your CD collection, and put on a nice snappy bluegrass song. Tap along with the rhythm and when you get that coordinated with the recording, say "TWO" when your foot comes up. Now you're ready to try it on your mandolin. You'll want to play the chop only on the TWO. So tap your foot, go to a G chord, and smack, whack, or chop down on the strings only on the TWO beat. Now you've got the chop where you want it.

PLAYING CHORDS WITH THE MELODY. When you're first playing the melody of a song, you can ignore the chords written above the lines. After you're comfortable playing the melody, you can play partial chords as a harmony to the melody notes. For example, look at "Angel Band," on page 19. In measure number 1, the first melody note is a "D" and above that is a G chord. Instead of just hitting the "D" note by its lonesome, you can play any note of a G chord that's on a string next to the "D." So, you've got two choices. You can play the G string open or the A string at the second fret. The easiest, and best sounding choice would be to play the open G string with the D melody note. There! You're playing harmony.

Some of the songs in the book include one or several numbers after the chords. These numbers represent harmony chord positions which you'll find on pages 76-77. Any time you play a note, you can also play a harmony of that note. The Harmony Chord Positions page show you some harmony note possibilites. A black dot on the chords indicates the 5th or 7th fret. An x means that you don't play that string.

Amazing Grace

No hymn can rival "Amazing Grace" in popularity. The composer of the lyrics was John Newton, who was born in England in 1725. When he was nine, his mother died, and he was shipped off to sea as a cabin boy. He later deserted the British navy and was whipped and put in irons. Rising through the ranks, he eventually became captain of a slave ship. During a violent storm, Newton found solace in God and he later left the sea to become an ordained minister of the Church of England. After composing the lyrics to "Amazing Grace" in 1789, Newton set the words to an anonymous tune that often appears in old hymn books as "New Britain" or "Harmony Grove."

It's a good thing for us that John Newton named this classic hymn "Amazing Grace" because it comes at the front of the alphabet, and it's easier to start pickin' on a tune you already know and love.

The first thing you should notice about "Amazing Grace" is that it's in 3/4, or waltz, time. That means there are three beats per measure and the rhythm sounds like "ONE, two-three, ONE, two-three." Before you start, take a look at the chart on the top right hand corner of this page. This handy diagram will tell you exactly which notes will be used to play "Amazing Grace." Notice that we'll be using our index finger to play B and E and our ring finger to play the G and high D. Let your middle and pinky fingers rest for now.

ICE COLD LICKS: First, play the unadorned melody as written on the facing page. Remember that every note with a single vertical line attached to it gets one beat. If there is a double line, that note gets two beats. If there's a dot after a note, it gets half again the value of the note preceding it. For example, measure 7 will get three beats because it has a dotted double line.

WARM LICKS: After you can play the simple melody of "Amazing Grace," you're ready to juice up the rhythm a little. Of course, this isn't the kind of tune you want to go crazy with, so please try to restrain yourself. "Amazing Grace" is the perfect tune to try the Tremolo, which is the "mother" of all mandolin licks. (See page 73). You can use the Tremolo on any of the notes EXCEPT the 8th notes (which are tied together like the B and G in measure 1.)

Harmony Notes

All the melody notes of "Amazing Grace" are on the D or A strings. To play the harmony of any melody note on the D string, simply play the G string open along with the melody note. For melody notes on the A string, you'll find the harmony by playing the D string open.

Amazing Grace

Tempo: Respectfully Slow

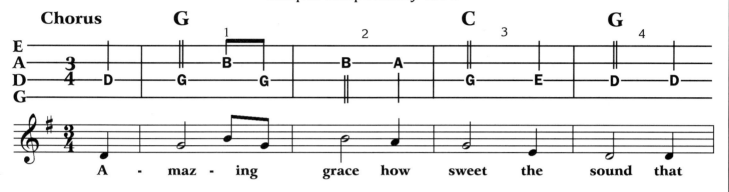

A - maz - ing grace how sweet the sound that

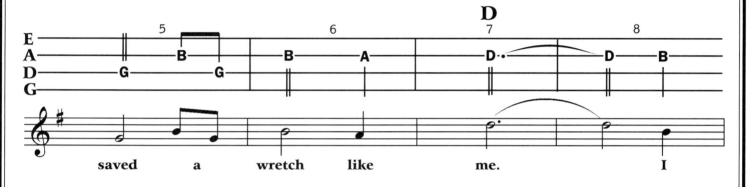

saved a wretch like me. I

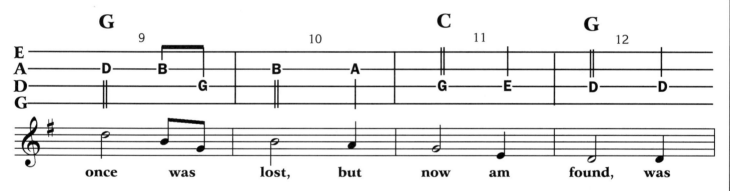

once was lost, but now am found, was

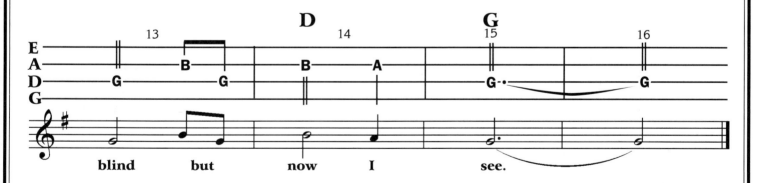

blind but now I see.

Note: The chords (G, C & D) are optional when you're new at playing the melody. Later on, you can add harmony chord positions (p. 76). For example, in measure 7 you can play the D6 harmony chord position. How do you figure out which harmony chord to play? Pick a harmony note that's on a string next to the melody note.

Angel Band

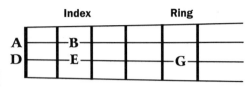

Although its original title was "My Latest Sun is Sinking Fast," this hymn has also been published under the title "The Land of Beulah." It was composed in 1860 by Jefferson Hascall and William Bradbury and it first appeared in J.D. Dadmun's *Melodeon*. Born in York, Maine, on October 6, 1816, Bradbury became an organist, piano teacher and singing-school master as well as a prolific composer and compiler of sacred books. His nine hundred hymns and fifty-nine books sold more than two million copies. "Angel Band" was first recorded by Smith's Sacred Singers on April 17, 1928 in Atlanta, Georgia. It acquired new fame when The Stanley Brothers' 1955 Mercury recording was played in the closing credits of the 2000 film, *O Brother, Where Art Thou?*

"Angel Band" has all the same ingredients as "Amazing Grace." Both are gospel songs in 3/4 or waltz time, both use only the G, C and D chords, and both use the same five melody notes: D, E, G, A and B.

ICE COLD LICKS: Just play the melody, in all its glory. Remember that the half notes have two lines attached to them and get two beats each. You can play each half note once and let it ring for two beats or play two quarter notes.

COOL LICKS: Apply the Tremolo to any or all of the half notes. (See page 73.)

HOT LICKS on HALF NOTES: The half notes give you further opportunities to improvise. On any of the half notes, you can use the Half Note Rhythm #1: **ONE**-TWO, ONE or **DOWN**-UP, DOWN with your pick or Half Note Rhythm #2: **ONE**-TWO, ONE-TWO or **DOWN**-UP, DOWN-UP with your pick. (See page 75.)

NOTE: The HOT LICKS on HALF NOTES can be used on any half note in this book, such as in "Amazing Grace," "House of the Rising Sun," or "Knoxville Girl."

Harmony Notes

All the melody notes of "Angel Band" are on the D or A strings. To play the harmony of any melody note on the D string, simply play the G string open. For melody notes on the A string, you'll find the harmony by playing the D string open.

Key of G

Angel Band

Tempo: Medium Slow

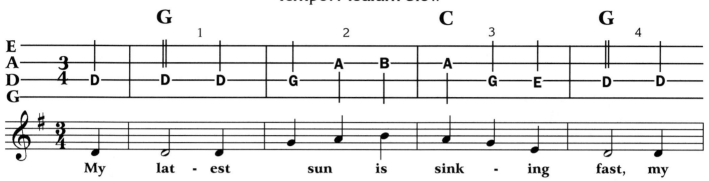

My lat - est sun is sink - ing fast, my

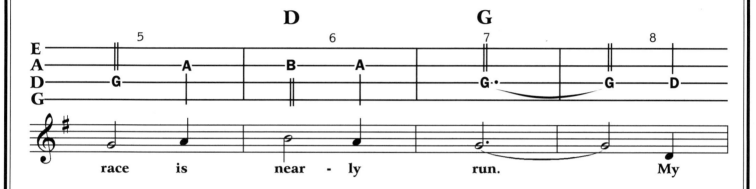

race is near - ly run. My

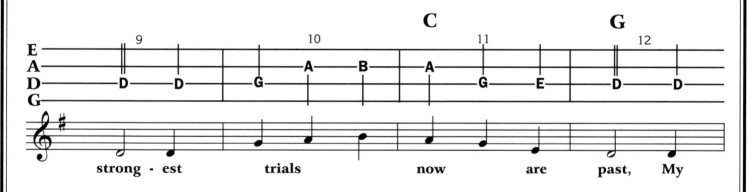

strong - est trials now are past, My

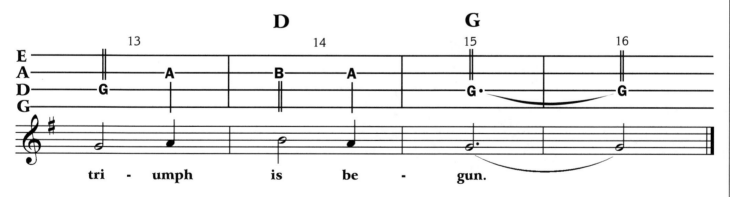

tri - umph is be - gun.

CHORUS:

D   **G**
Oh come, angel band,

D   **G**
Come and around me stand,

   C   **G**
Oh, bear me away on your snowy wings,

   D   **G**
To my immortal home,

   C   **G**
Oh bear me away on your snowy wings

   D   **G**
To my immortal home.

Cryin' Holy Unto the Lord

The Carter Family called this song "On the Rock Where Moses Stood" when they recorded it in Memphis, Tennessee, on November 24, 1930, but the song can be traced to African-American sources much earlier. Bill Monroe recorded it in Atlanta, Georgia, on October 7, 1940, but Monroe's version is suspiciously similar to that of Wade Mainer & The Sons of The Mountaineers, who recorded it on February 4, 1939.

	Index	Middle		Ring	
A	B♭	B	C		D
D		E			G

ICE COLD LICKS: This slightly spooky melody awaits you. Notice that in measures 5 and 6 you'll be playing a B flat, which is the A string fretted at the first fret with your index finger. In measures 2, 4, and 8, there is a dotted half note, which gets three beats.

WARM LICKS: On any of the half notes, you can play the Gallop, as shown on the Mandolin Rhythms on page 73. Since each Gallop takes up one quarter note, and there are two quarter notes in a half note, for each half note, you can play the Gallop twice. On the dotted half notes in measures 2 and 4, you can play the Gallop three times.

HOT LICKS: In addition to the Gallop on the half notes, you can also use the Porcupine (page 73) and/or the Watermelon (page 74).

Jack Shelton, Tiny Dotson, Wade Mainer, Howard Dixon

Harmony Notes

All the melody notes in "Crying Holy Unto the Lord" are on the D or A strings. To play the harmony of any melody note on the D string, simply play the G string open. For melody notes on the A string, you'll find the harmony by playing the D string open.

Key of G

Cryin' Holy Unto the Lord

Tempo: Pretty Perky

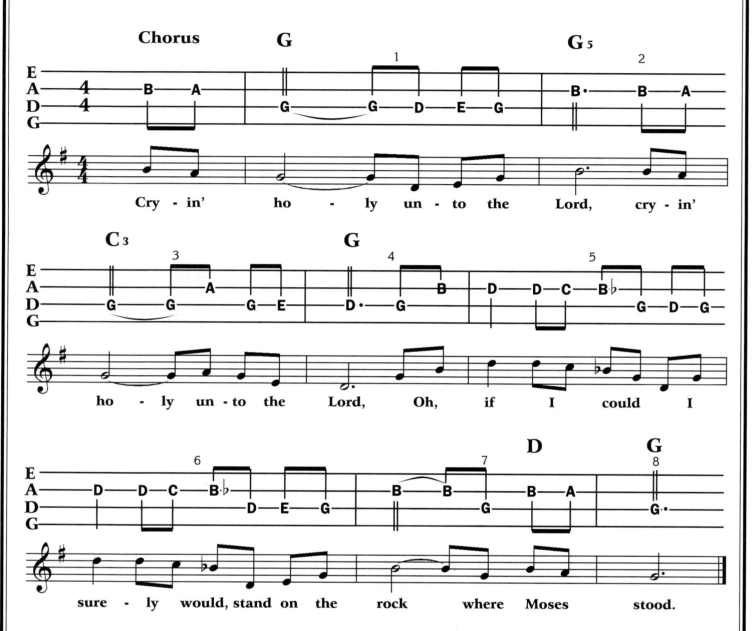

Cry - in' ho - ly un - to the Lord, cry - in'

ho - ly un - to the Lord, Oh, if I could I

sure - ly would, stand on the rock where Moses stood.

Sinners, run (sinners, run) and hide your face (and hide your face),
Sinners, run (sinners, run) and hide your face (and hide your face),
Go run unto the rocks and hide your face
For I ain't (Lord, Lord) no stranger now. (Chorus)

Lord, I ain't (Lord, I ain't) no stranger now (no stranger now),
Lord, I ain't (Lord, I ain't) no stranger now (no stranger now),
I been introduced to the Father and the Son
And I ain't (Lord, Lord) no stranger now. (Chorus)

Note: In measures 1, 3 and 7 there is a curved line called a "tie." The tie tells you to pick only the first of the two notes tied together. However, when you're playing the Gallop, Porcupine or Watermelon licks, you DO play the second note of the two notes that are tied together.

Don't This Road Look Rough & Rocky

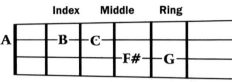

Searching for clues to the origin of "Don't This Road Look Rough and Rocky" is like trying to untangle a knot in a fisherman's net. Some of the strands that make up this song come from such diverse songs such as "My Dear Companion," "Fond Affection" and "Don't Forget Me Little Darling." In 1927, Sigmund Spaeth published a fragment of the song in his book *Weep Some More, My Lady* under the title "Go and Leave Me if You Wish To." In his book, *Ozark Folksongs*, Vance Randolph found some ten additional songs that share pieces of "Don't This Road Look Rough And Rocky." The Blue Sky Boys recorded it as "Can't You Hear Those Night Birds Singing." For fans of bluegrass, it was Flatt & Scruggs' May 19, 1954, recording that helped solidify this version of the song.

ICE COLD LICKS: You'll find all the melody notes of this song on the D and A strings. In music lingo, the first note in measure one is a dotted quarter note. That means it gets one and a half beats. Your foot would go DOWN-UP-DOWN on the G note. The second note in measure one, an A with a "flag," is an eighth note. Your foot just finished the G note on the DOWN, so this eighth note would get an UP with your foot.

WARM LICKS: At the end of line two on measures 7 and 8, you've got two half notes of A. This would be a perfect place to play the Tremolo for four beats. (See page 73).

HOT LICKS: On measures 1, 5, 9, and 13 you'll notice a dotted quarter followed by an eighth note. Instead of just letting the dotted quarter note ring for one and a half beats, you can play the Going t' Town Lick (page 74).

Photo by Wayne Erbsen

Well Bucket

Harmony Notes

All the melody notes are on the D or A strings. To play the harmony of any melody note on the D string, simply play the G string open. For melody notes on the A string, you'll find the harmony by playing the D string open.

Don't This Road Look Rough & Rocky

Key of G   Tempo: Second Gear

Dar - ling,   I   have   come   to   tell   you,

Though   it   al - most   breaks   my   heart,

That   be - fore   the   morn-ing   dar - ling,

We'll   be   many   miles   a - part.

CHORUS: **C** Don't this road look rough and rocky?   **G**

D Don't that sea look wide and deep?

G Don't my baby seem the sweetest

D When she's in my arms   **G** asleep?

23

Down the Road

It never fails that "Down the Road" is a hit with my mandolin students. That's because it's one of those songs that simply sounds great, and that's how we're going to play it: simply. The first bluegrass version of this tune was the hot 1950s recording by Flatt & Scruggs, but they didn't sing a chorus. In the early 1960s, the Greenbriar Boys came along and added a chorus, which they probably made up. The song is actually much older than the Flatt & Scruggs recording. Uncle Dave Macon recorded a rousing rendition on July 25, 1928, that he called "Over the Road I'm Bound to Go." The melody is basically the same as the tune "Ida Red," which was first recorded by Fiddlin' Powers & Family on August 19, 1924.

ICE COLD LICKS: Just play the melody. Be sure to play the quarter notes with a DOWN stroke and each pair of eighth notes with a DOWN-UP stroke of your pick.

WARM LICKS: After you're comfortable playing the basic melody of "Down the Road," you're ready to use the mandolin rhythm I call the "Watermelon." I call it that because it has four quick 16th notes that correspond to the four syllables of the word "wa-ter-mel-on." Besides that, I've been eating my share of watermelons lately.

Let me show you how the Watermelon works. Look at the first four notes of "Down the Road, " which are G, G, G and E — all quarter notes played on the D string. Since each quarter note gets one beat, tap your foot four times and say out loud, "G, G, G, E." Every time you say one of the letters, your foot should hit the floor and come up. Now tap your foot four times again, this time saying "watermelon," with each foot tap. To play the Watermelon on "Down the Road," fret the D string at the fifth fret, which will give you a G. With your pick, go DOWN-UP, DOWN-UP three times on the G note and one time on the E. Congratulations, you've just played four Watermelons.

HOT LICKS: Once you get the Watermelon under control in measure 1, you can use it to play on any or all of the quarter notes in this or practically any song. Even better, you can alternate the Watermelon with any quarter note. For example, on the first four notes of measure 1, try alternating the Watermelon with just a single note, which for fun we'll call a "Spam." First, say "Watermelon, Spam, Watermelon, Spam," tapping your foot once for each word. Then play it that way on the mandolin. When you can do that, reverse it, saying and then playing "Spam, Watermelon, Spam, Watermelon." Presto! You're improvising.

RED HOT LICKS: You can use Echo Notes to dress up the naked quarter notes of "Down the Road." Any time the melody is a G on the D string, you can play an open G as a drone. On the E notes you can also play the G as a drone. (Page 74.)

Down the Road

Tempo: Bouncy

Chorus

Down the road, down the road, I've got a sugar babe down the road.

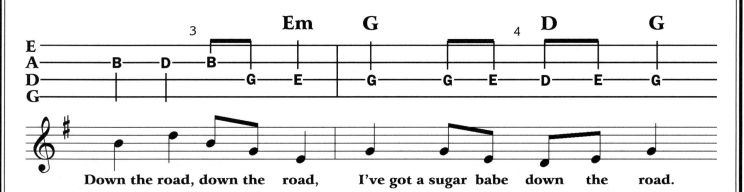

Down the road, down the road, I've got a sugar babe down the road.

Down the road about a mile or two
Lives a little girl named Pearly Blue.
About so high and her hair is brown,
Prettiest thing, boys, in this town. (Chorus)

Anytime you want to know
Where I'm going down the road.
Get my girl on the line,
You can find me there most anytime. (Chorus)

Every day and Sunday too
I go see my Pearly Blue.
Soon as you hear the rooster crow,
You can see me heading down the road. (Chorus)

Every time I get the blues
I walk the soles right off my shoes.
Don't know why I love her so,
That gal of mine lives down the road. (Chorus)

Harmony Notes

All the melody notes of "Down the Road" are on the D or A strings. To play the harmony of any melody note on the D string, simply play the G string open. For melody notes on the A string, you'll find the harmony by playing the D string open.

East Virginia

Before printed music and phonograph records essentially froze versions of songs, even singers who were practically neighbors often sang radically different versions of the same song. "East Virginia" is a good example of a song in which each early version is markedly different from the next. One of the first to record it was B.F. Shelton, who called his version "Oh Molly Dear," when he waxed it for Ralph Peer of RCA Victor on July 29, 1927. His rendition borrowed heavily from the family of songs usually entitled "Silver Dagger" and also "Columbus Stockade Blues." Clarence Ashley, who lived in the same general area as B.F. Shelton, was the next to record it, in February, 1930. He called it "Dark Holler Blues." By the time the Carter Family recorded it in 1934 and again in 1935, the song had lost its haunting flavor and was done in a more foursquare manner. Karl and Harty recorded it on October 7, 1936, as "Darling, Think of What You've Done." "East Virginia," or whichever name you prefer to call it, seems to have its deepest roots in 17th century England. Cecil Sharp collected it under the title "Ole Virginny," in Harlan County, Kentucky in 1917 when he came to the Southeast from England in 1916-1918 to collect British ballads.

ICE COLD LICKS: The melody of "East Virginia," is simply a great song to play simply.

Bill Monroe

WARM LICKS: You'll notice that on measures 5 and 9, the melody goes up to the E string, and the note preceding the E note is a D played on the A string at the fifth fret. When it comes time to hit the E note, try hitting the D note again and slide UP on the A string to the seventh fret, which produces an E note. Once at the seventh fret of the A string, you can then play BOTH the A string at the seventh fret and the E string open. Amazing!

HOT LICKS: On "East Virginia," I would most likely rely on the Watermelon lick and sometimes the Gallop. Remember that on the half notes on measures 1, 5, 7-8, 9, 13 and 15, you can play either of these rhythms twice.

Harmony Notes

You'll find all the melody notes of "East Virginia" on the E, A and D strings. To play the harmony of any melody note on the A string, simply play the D string open. When the melody is on the D string, the harmony note is the G string played open. On the notes where the melody is played on the E string, see WARM LICKS, above.

East Virginia

Tempo: An Easy Lope

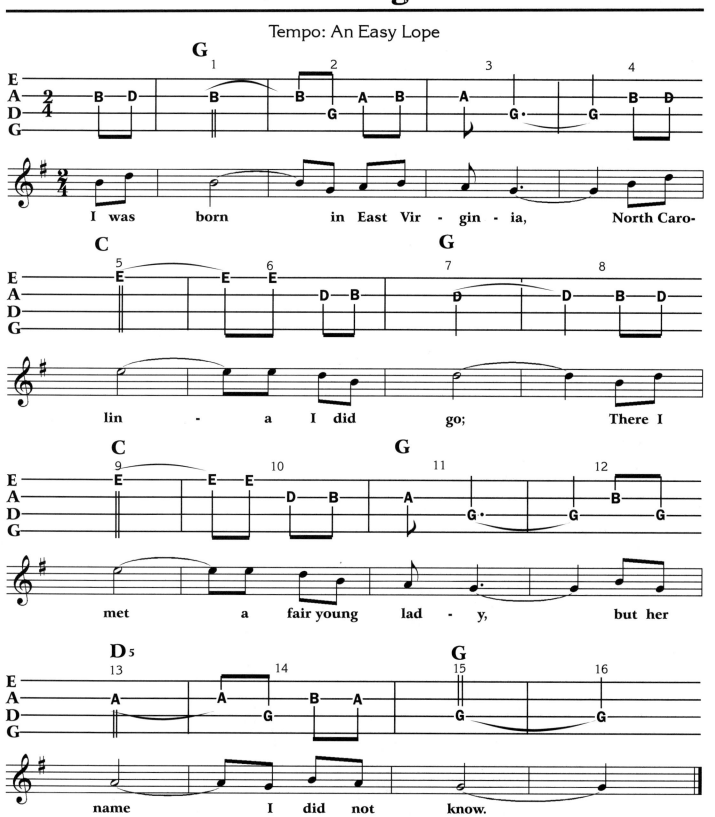

Oh, her hair was dark in color,
And her lips were ruby red,
On her breast she wore white linen,
There I longed to lay my head.

I'd rather be in some dark holler,
Where the sun don't ever shine
Than to see you with another,
And to know you'll never be mine.

Handsome Molly

Sung under such titles as "Loving Hannah," "Hannah My Love," "The Lover's Lament," "The Irish Girl," and even "Pretty Polly," this song was first recorded by G.B. Grayson and Henry Whitter on October 10, 1927. The Stanley Brothers recorded it for King records on January 16, 1961. This version is from the CD, *Rural Roots of Bluegrass,* as sung by Laura Boosinger and Wayne Erbsen.

ICE COLD LICKS. Play just the straight-ahead melody of "Handsome Molly."

WARM LICKS: Instead of playing the A string open at the end of measure 2, you can add a slide. When you finish playing the G note in measure 2, simply slide the G from the fifth fret to the seventh fret, which will produce an A note. As is often the case in situations like this, you can then play the D string fretted at the seventh fret along with the A string open.

HOT LICKS: If you like, you can add the Going t' Town lick on the D notes of measure 1. Instead of playing the quarter notes in measures 2, 3 and 4 you can simply play Going t' as you can hear on track 37 of the CD.

Photo by Wayne Erbsen

Key of G

Handsome Molly

Tempo: Half Fast

Sailing 'round the o - cean, sailing 'round the sea,

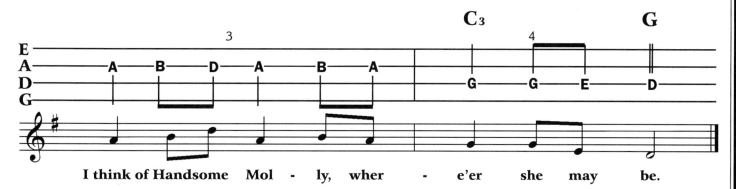

I think of Handsome Mol - ly, wher - e'er she may be.

I wish I were in London, or some other seaport town,
I'd set my foot on a steamship and I'd sail the ocean 'round. (Chorus)

Do you remember, Molly, when you gave me your right hand?
You said if you ever married that I would be that man.
   I would be that man, Oh, I would be that man
   You said if you ever married that I would be that man.

I saw you in church on Sunday, there you passed me by,
I could tell your heart was changing by the roving of your eye.
   Roving of your eye, by the roving of your eye
   I could tell your heart was changing by the roving of your eye.

Her hair was dark as a raven, her eyes were dark as coal,
Her cheeks shone like the lilies out in the morning glow.
   Out in the morning glow, out in the morning glow
   Her cheeks shone like the lilies out in the morning glow.

So go on handsome Molly, and marry who you please,
While my poor heart is breaking, you're going at your ease.
   Going at your ease, you're going at your ease
   While my poor heart is breaking, you're going at your ease.

Harmony Notes

In "Handsome Molly," the melody is played entirely on the D and A strings. For the melody notes played on the D string, the harmony is the G string played open. When the melody is on the A string, the harmony is the D string open.

John Hardy

It was payday night at the Shawnee Coal Company in McDowell County, West Virginia, in 1893. John Hardy was celebrating by gambling and drinking heavily. During the crap game, John laid his pistol on the table and solemnly spoke to his gun, "Now, I want you to lay there. The first man that steals money from me, I mean to kill him." About midnight he began to lose and claimed that one of the players had stolen twenty-five cents from him. Denying that he had taken the money, the accused man took one look at John Hardy's weapon and gave him twenty-five cents. With that, John Hardy said, "Don't you know that I won't lie to my gun?" and shot the man dead. The killer was soon captured by Sheriff John Effler and deputy John Campbell. Sentenced to die, John Hardy stood on the gallows on January 19, 1894, and renounced the evils of gambling and whiskey. The lyrics of this song were first printed on April 29, 1924, in *The Sunday Advertiser*, Huntington, West Virginia.

	Index	Middle		Ring
E — F				
A	B	C		D
D	E		F#	G

ICE COLD LICKS: You'll find the basic melody of "John Hardy" pretty easy because the song is built on a four note phrase that you'll see in measures 1, 3, and 5. Another bonus is the fact that measures 2 and 6 are also identical. Note that in measure 1 we're using an F instead of the more common F#.

HOT LICKS: On any of the quarter notes you can play the Porcupine, the Gallop, or the Watermelon rhythms. Or better yet, you can mix up all three.

NOTE: The D in measure 4 with the four vertical lines is a whole note, which you can think of as four quarter notes, which means you could play any of the rhythms I just mentioned four times.

Photo by Wayne Erbsen

John Hardy

Tempo: Pretty Snappy

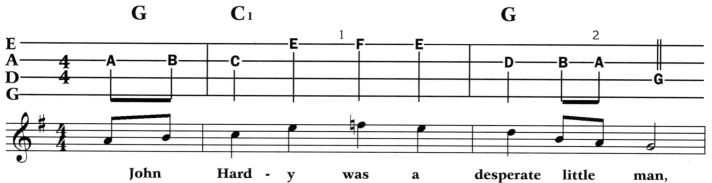

John Hard - y was a desperate little man,

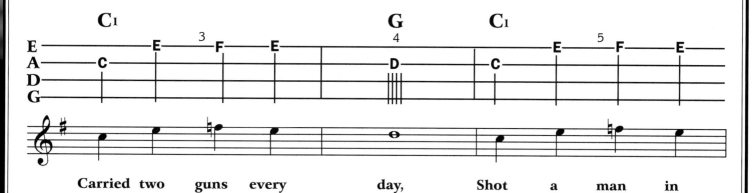

Carried two guns every day, Shot a man in

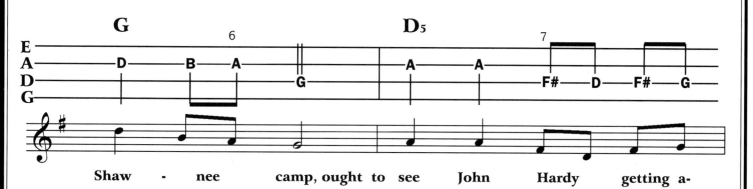

Shaw - nee camp, ought to see John Hardy getting a-

way, poor boy, see John Hardy getting a - way.

John Hardy was standing at the barroom door
Showing no interest in the game.
Up stepped a woman with a dollar in her hand;
Saying, "Deal John Hardy in the game, poor boy,
Deal John Hardy in the game."

Keep on the Sunny Side of Life

	Index	Middle	Ring
E			
A	B—C—		—D—
D	—E—	—F#—	—G—

No song is more associated with the Carter Family than "Keep on the Sunny Side of Life." Although it was considered their theme song, it was actually composed in 1899 with lyrics by Ada Blenkhorn and music by J. Howard Entwisle. Blenkhorn was inspired to write the words when her invalid cousin insisted that she push his wheel chair down "the sunny side of the street."

Even though the song was recorded as early as 1910 on a cylinder, it was the Carter Family who made it popular. They recorded it at their second session for Victor on May 9, 1928, and again on May 8, 1935, for the American Record Company. Given the song's wide popularity, it is interesting that it has not been recorded more often. Perhaps its close association with the Carter Family has dimmed its appeal to other recording artists. Whatever the reason, let's pick it!

ICE COLD LICKS: You'll find "Keep on the Sunny Side of Life" pretty straightforward to play. There's nothing quirky about the timing or the choice of notes, so this song should fall easily under the magic of your fingers.

COOL LICKS: "Keep on the Sunny Side of Life" is the perfect song to strut your Porcupine lick (page 73). You can play one Porcupine for each quarter note. In measure 3, you can play the Porcupine twice, since the half note is the same as two quarter notes (this is HIGHER MATH).

HOT LICKS: On any of the quarter notes, alternate your Gallop with your Porcupine licks.

Harmony Notes

All the melody notes of "Keep on the Sunny Side of Life" are found on the D, A or E strings. When the melody is on the D string, you can play the G string open as a harmony note. On melody notes that are found on the A string, the harmony is the D string open.

"Keep on The Sunny Side" - A.P. Carter's epitaph

Key of G — Keep on the Sunny Side of Life

Tempo: March-Like

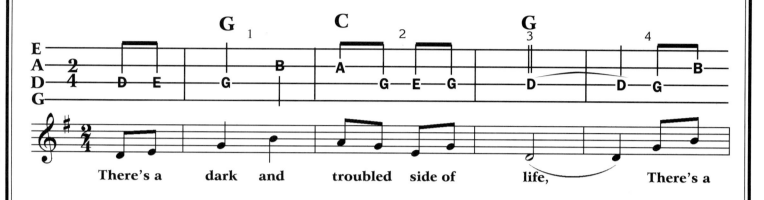

There's a   dark   and   troubled   side of   life,   There's a

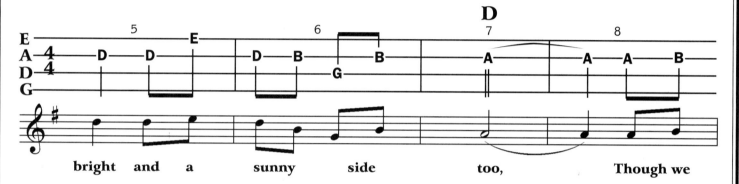

bright   and   a   sunny   side   too,   Though we

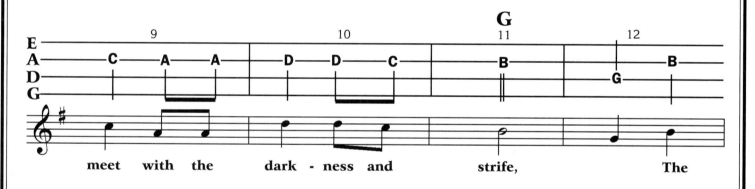

meet   with   the   dark - ness   and   strife,   The

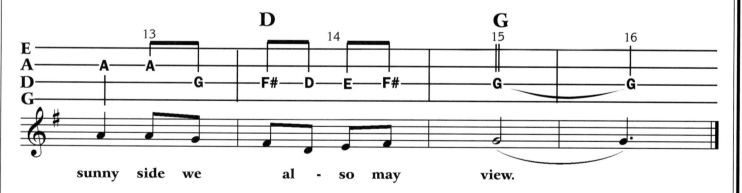

sunny   side   we   al - so   may   view.

CHORUS: Keep on the sunny side always on the sunny side,
Keep on the sunny side of life,
It will help us every day it will brighten all our way,
If we keep on the sunny side of life.

33

Little Maggie

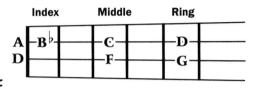

Index   Middle   Ring

Second cousin once removed to "Little Maggie" is another feisty mountain woman named "Darling Cory." In fact, both songs often share some of the same verses. On October 12, 1923, Charles L. Miller of Waycross, Georgia, reported he'd heard this song in railroad and construction camps in West Virginia, Virginia and Tennessee. One of Miller's verses goes, "Wake up little Maggie!/ What makes you sleep so sound?/ The highway robbers are raging,/ And the sun is almost down." Now considered a bluegrass standard, "Little Maggie" was first recorded by Grayson & Whitter on August 1, 1928. Wade Mainer and Zeke Morris recorded it next, on August 2, 1937. In 1948, the Stanley Brothers recorded it on Rich-R-Tone.

ICE COLD LICKS: The spooky melody of "Little Maggie," doesn't need decoration to make it sound right. Notice that you'll be playing several Fs (D string at the third fret) and B flats, (A string at the first fret.) Be sure to add some of the harmony notes described in the box below.

WARM LICKS: The Porcupine lick fits "Little Maggie" like a glove. You can use this prickly lick on any quarter note. The Gallop also works well and you can alternate between these two rhythms.

Photo by Wayne Erbsen

Harmony Notes

All the melody notes of "Little Maggie" are on the D or A strings. To play the harmony of any melody note on the D string, simply play the A string open. For melody notes on the A string, you'll find the harmony by playing the D string open.

Little Maggie

Tempo: Not Too Fast

Oh, how can I ever stand it
To see those two blue eyes;
They're shining in the moonlight
Like two diamonds in the sky.

I'm going down to the station
With my suitcase in my hand;
I'm going to leave this country
I'm going to some far and distant land.

Go 'way, go 'way little Maggie,
Go and do the best you can.
I'll get me another woman
You can get you another man.

My Home's Across the Blue Ridge Mtns.

As far back as 1909, this song was collected by Louise Rand Bascom as "My Own True Love." In August of 1925, it was recorded by Kelly Harrell and Henry Whitter under the title "I'm Going Back to North Carolina." The Carolina Tar Heels apparently renamed the song "My Home's Across the Blue Ridge Mountains" when they journeyed to the Okeh studios in Camden, New Jersey, for their 1929 recording session. In the 1930s it was recorded under this title by the Carter Family, Fiddlin' Arthur Smith and the Delmore Brothers. Over the years, the song has also been titled "My Home's Across the Smoky Mountains." Whatever you call it, it's a great traditional bluegrass song that's both fun and easy to play.

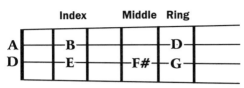

ICE COLD LICKS: Helping to make this easy to play is the fact that the first and third lines of the song are practically identical.

HOT LICKS: Measure 1 and measure 5 start with B quarter notes connected by a tie to a B eighth note. Another way of writing this would have been to make those Bs into a dotted quarter note. If you think of it like that, then you can substitute a Going t' Town lick (page 74) for the dotted quarter note.

RED HOT LICK: You can play the Watermelon lick once for each quarter note you find in this song. Since two quarter notes equal a half note, you can play the Watermelon lick twice for each half note.

Mars Hill College

Harmony Notes
All the melody notes of "My Home's Across the Blue Ridge Mountains" are on the D or A strings. To play the harmony of any melody note on the D string, simply play the G string open. For melody notes on the A string, you'll find the harmony by playing the D string open.

My Home's Across the Blue Ridge Mtns.

Key of G

Tempo: Third Gear

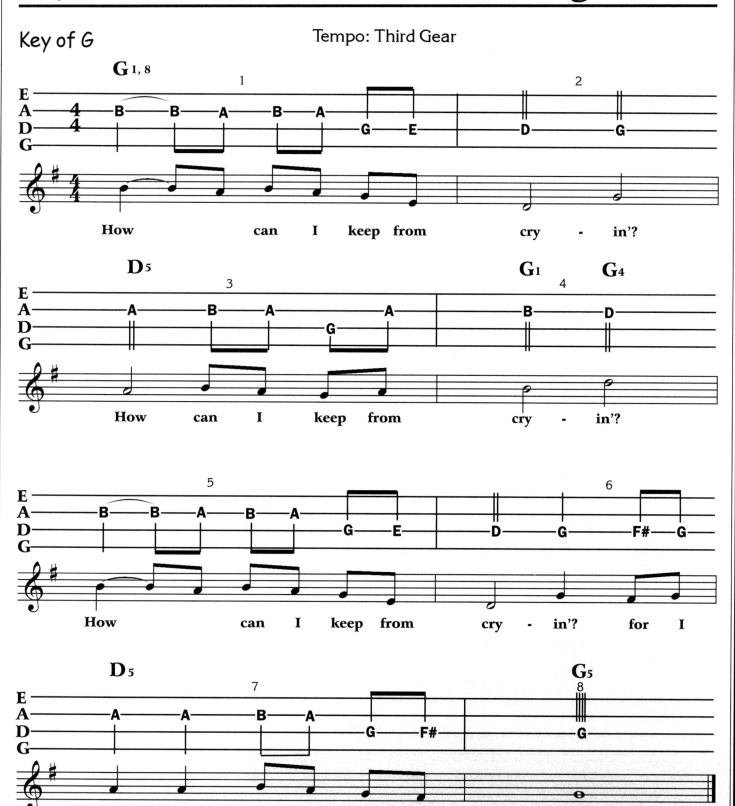

CHORUS:

My home's across the Blue Ridge Mountains,
My home's across the Blue Ridge Mountains,
My home's across the Blue Ridge Mountains,
And I never expect to see you anymore.

Rock and feed my baby candy,
Rock and feed my baby candy,
Rock and feed my baby candy,
And I never expect to see you anymore.

Nine Pound Hammer

O n the short list of bluegrass favorites, "Nine Pound Hammer" can be traced to the May 13, 1927, recording in New York by Al Hopkins & His Buckle Busters. Apparently, the band put the song together in Brunswick's New York studio out of what fragments the band members could remember. The tune bears more than a passing similarity to "Swannanoa Town," collected in 1916 by Cecil Sharp. There is, in fact, an entire chapter devoted to "Nine Pound Hammer" in Green's 1972 book *Only a Miner*.

ICE COLD LICKS: The melody of "Nine Pound Hammer" is pretty straightforward, especially if you listen to the CD. This tune uses a lot of ties, which are the curved lines that connect two notes. When you see two notes connected by a tie, play only the first note and let that note ring.

NOTE: "Nine Pound Hammer" uses one little rhythmic figure over and over that consists of a half note tied to an eighth note. You'll see this in measures 1-2, 5-6, 7-8, 9-10, 13-14 and 15-16. On each half note your foot would go DOWN-UP, DOWN-UP. The eighth note would get one DOWN.

WARM LICKS: On any of the half notes, you can play the Gallop twice, the Watermelon twice and/or the Porcupine twice.

Harmony Notes

All the melody notes of "Nine Pound Hammer" are on the D or A strings. To play the harmony of any melody note on the D string, simply play the G string open. For melody notes on the A string, you'll find the harmony by playing the D string open.

Nine Pound Hammer

Tempo: Snappy

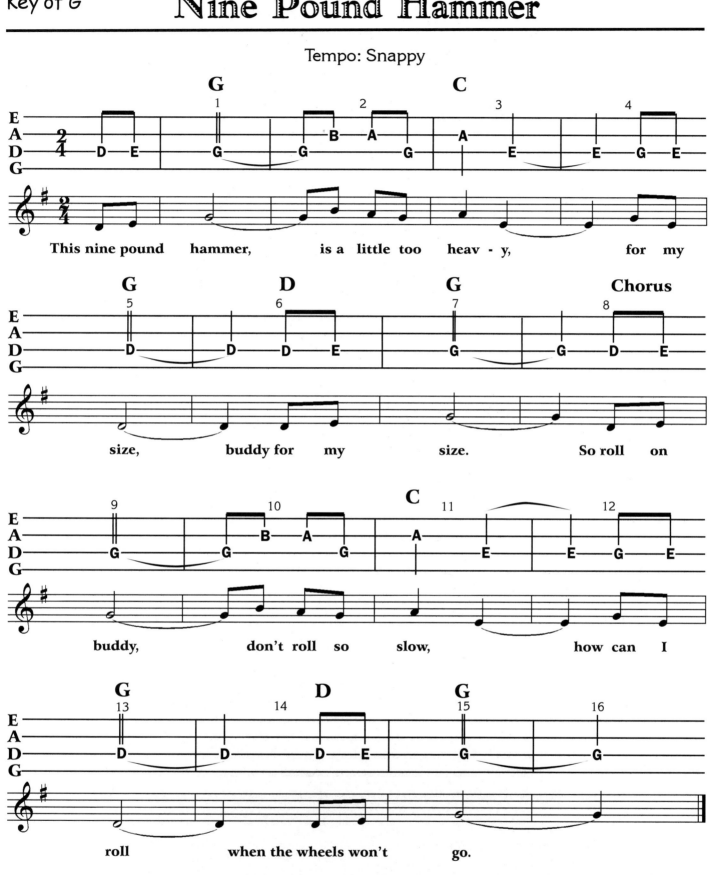

Somebody stole my nine pound hammer,
Baby, took it and gone, baby took it and gone. (Chorus)

Goin' on a mountain, see my baby,
Ain't comin' back, no I ain't comin' back. (Chorus)

Roll in My Sweet Baby's Arms

	Index	Middle	Ring
A	B	C	
D	E		F#	G

It was Buster Carter & Preston Young's June 26, 1931, recording that distilled this song into a blue-grass classic. The Monroe Brothers apparently learned it from this 78 record, and recorded it on October 12, 1936. Lester Flatt heard the song when he worked with Charlie Monroe and recorded it with Earl Scruggs on October 20, 1950.

ICE COLD LICKS: The melody of "Roll in My Sweet Baby's Arms" is simple enough, but the timing is not as straightforward as many bluegrass songs. In measure 3 you'll find an E note with a "flag," which is an eighth note. Eighth notes get a half a beat, or a Down with your foot. The G after it is a dotted quarter note, which gets one and a half beats, or Up Down Up. A careful listen to the CD that accompanies this book will fix you up.

WARM LICKS: You can slide into the A note in measure 7 as we've done before. After you hit the last G note in measure 6, simply hit the G again and slide on the D string from the fifth to the seventh fret.

HOT LICKS: Since this tune is supposed to be played pretty fast, I'd probably stick with the Watermelon lick on the quarter notes.

Courtesy of Doug Walker

Harmony Notes

All the melody notes of "Roll in My Sweet Baby's Arms" are on the D or A strings. To play the harmony of any melody note on the D string, simply play the G string open. For melody notes on the A string, you'll find the harmony by playing the D string open.

40

Roll in My Sweet Baby's Arms

Key of G

Tempo: Wide Open

CHORUS:

Roll in my sweet baby's arms,
Roll in my sweet baby's arms,
Lay 'round the shack
'Til the mail train comes back,
And I'll roll in my sweet baby's arms.

They tell me her parents do not like me,
They have drove me away from the door,
If I had all my time to go over,
I would never go back any more.

Shady Grove

This old Appalachian folk song is a standard both in old-time and in bluegrass music. Old-time musicians commonly use one of two melodies for this tune. One is in the key of A minor and bears more than a passing resemblance to the old English ballad entitled "Matty Groves." The other is played in the key of A major. Starting in the 1940s, Bill Monroe featured "Shady Grove" in live performances using a melody associated with "Fly Around My Pretty Little Miss" and "Western Country." Monroe's version was possibly influenced by the Prairie Ramblers, who performed "Shady Grove" in the 1930s while on the National Barn Dance radio show based in Chicago. The Monroe Brothers were also featured on the show, as dancers, not musicians, strangely enough. Bill Monroe eventually recorded a fast version of "Shady Grove" in Nashville, Tennessee, on November 10, 1961, at the same session he recorded "Nine Pound Hammer."

ICE COLD LICKS: The melody that we're going to play is similar to Bill Monroe's version, and you should find it quite easy. Make sure to use your index finger to play the B and E notes, your middle finger on the F# note, and your ring finger to play the G.

WARM LICKS: Scattered throughout "Shady Grove" are pairs of eighth notes. In fact, the song starts with a pair of eighth notes — the B and the A. Instead of playing any of the eighth notes as written, you can play two sixteenth notes. I call this a "Hot Dog." (See page 73.) Anywhere you like, you can substitute a Hot Dog for one, both, or none of the eighth notes. Try going through the song, adding the Hot Dog wherever you take the notion. There! You're improvising.

HOT LICKS: On any of the quarter notes, play either a Watermelon, a Gallop or even a Porcupine.

Bill Monroe, Monroe Fields, Joe Stuart

Photo by Martin Fox

Harmony Notes

All the melody notes of "Shady Grove" are on the D or A strings. To play the harmony of any melody note on the D note, simply play the G string open. For melody notes on the A string, you'll find the harmony by playing the D string open.

Shady Grove

Tempo: Pedal to the Metal

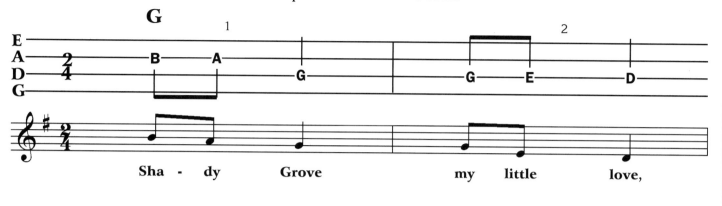

Sha - dy   Grove   my   little   love,

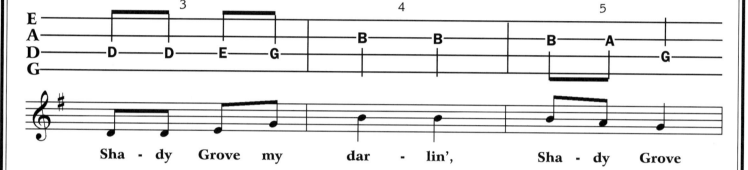

Sha - dy   Grove   my   dar - lin',   Sha - dy   Grove

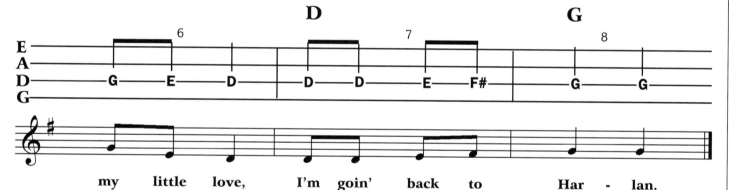

my   little   love,   I'm goin'   back   to   Har - lan.

I went to see my Shady Grove
Standing in the door.
Shoes and stockings in her hands,
Little bare feet on the floor.

Wished I had a big fat horse
Corn to feed him on.
Shady Grove to stay at home
Feed him while I'm gone.

Peaches in the summertime,
Apples in the fall.
If I can't get the girl I love
I won't have none at all.

The Lilly Brothers

43

Will the Circle Be Unbroken?

	Index	Middle		Ring	
A	B	C		D	
D	E			G	

The popularity of "Will the Circle Be Unbroken" can be traced to the Carter Family, who recorded it in New York City on May 6, 1935. The Carters based their song on an 1897 hymn with lyrics by Ada R. Habershon and melody by Charles H. Gabriel. Their recording kept intact the chorus and the melody of the original hymn, but used rewritten lyrics. While they were at it, they slapped an iron-clad copyright on it that prohibits reprinting their words in this book lest a swarm of bloodthirsty lawyers come calling at my door in the middle of the night. Since my mama didn't raise a fool, the lyrics that are provided are from the original 1897 song that are 100% in the public domain, thank you very much.

ICE COLD LICKS: The melody of "Will the Circle Be Unbroken," is one of the best-known tunes in bluegrass music, so I'm guessing you know it like the back of your hand. **56** After glancing at the first few notes of the music/tab, try to play it without looking at the book.

WARM LICKS: On any of the quarter notes, try playing the Watermelon. Remember that for every half note you can play the Watermelon **57** twice. For dotted half notes, you can play it three times.

HOT LICKS: Alternate the Gallop with the Porcupine on any of the quarter notes **58** and half notes.

Photo by Wayne Erbsen

Harmony Notes

All the melody notes of "Will the Circle Be Unbroken?" are on the D or A strings. To play the harmony of any melody note on the D string, simply play the G string open. For melody notes on the A string, you'll find the harmony by playing the D string open.

Will the Circle Be Unbroken?

Tempo: Medium Somber

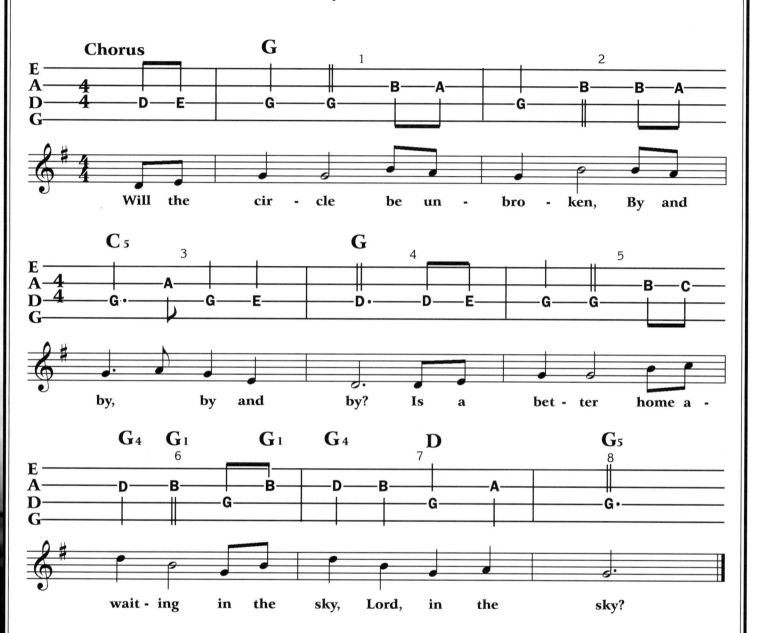

In the joyous days of childhood,
Oft they told of wondrous love
Pointed to the dying Saviour,
Now they dwell with Him above. (Chorus)

You remember songs of heaven,
Which you sang with childish voice,
Do you love the hymns they taught you,
Or are songs of earth your choice? (Chorus)

You can picture happy gatherings,
'Round the fireside long ago,
And you think of tearful partings,
When they left you here below. (Chorus)

One by one their seats were emptied,
One by one they went away,
Now the family is parted,
Will it be complete one day? (Chorus)

Playing in the Key of A

The key of A is a favorite of many old-time and bluegrass musicians. For us ignoramuses, the good news is that both the placement of the notes and the fingering are exactly the same for the key of A and also for the key of D, which we'll learn shortly. The only difference is that we'll start the A scale on the A string open, and the D scale on the D string open. Each scale uses the same fingering, except one string over from each other.

	Index		Middle	Ring
E	F#		G#	A
A	B		C#	D

The A Scale
A, B, C#, D, E, F#, G#, A

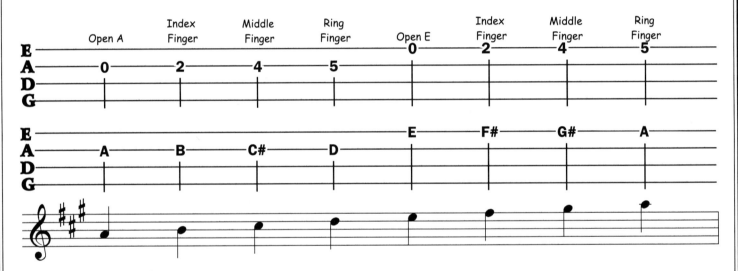

Many A tunes can be played using just the E and A strings. On some songs, however, you'll need the complete A scale, so here it is, in all its glory.

	Index		Middle	Ring
E	F#		G#	A
A	B		C#	D
D	E		F#	G#
	A		B	C#

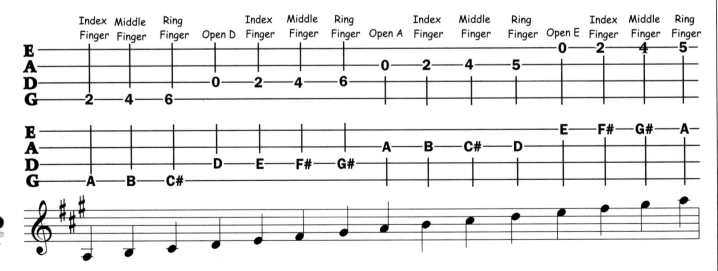

Cripple Creek

Tempo: Lickety Split

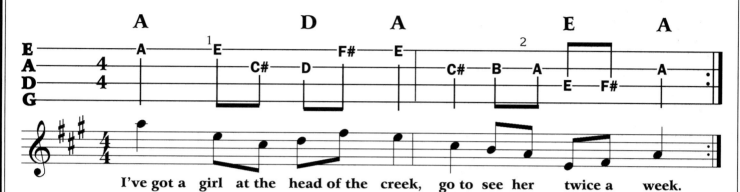

I've got a girl at the head of the creek, go to see her twice a week.

Chorus

Goin' up Cripple Creek goin' in a run, goin' up Cripple Creek have a little fun.

Here are all the notes you'll need to play "Cripple Creek.

	Index		Middle	Ring
E	F#			A
A	B		C#	D
	E		F#	

HOT LICKS: In the good old days, "Cripple Creek" was used as an old-time square dance tune, so you should play all the quarter notes with the Gallop, which will help to give it the dance feel of the old-time dance tune that it is.

62

ICE COLD LICKS: This melody will be easy to play, especially if you use your ring finger on the fifth fret, your middle finger on the fourth fret, and your index finger on the second fret.

61

NOTE: At the end of each line is a repeat sign, which means go back to the beginning and play that line again.

Harmony Notes

All the melody notes of "Cripple Creek" are on the A and E strings. To play the harmony of any melody note on the E string, simply play A string open. For melody notes on the A string, the harmony is the E string played open. The only exception is that when the melody is the D note on the A string, the harmony is the D string open.

House of the Rising Sun

A lthough I wouldn't stand here and tell you that "House of the Rising Sun" is a dyed-in-the-wool bluegrass song, it certainly has been done by a number of bluegrass bands. This just goes to show that pert' near any song can be done in bluegrass style. Heck, I know of a bluegrass band that did an entire record of Beatles songs, so there you have it.

	Index	Middle		Ring
E		G		A
A	B	C		D
	E			G

"Hamdolin" Photo by Wes Erbsen

There are several reasons I am including "House of the Rising Sun" in this book. First, I'm reasonably sure you've heard it numerous times and I'll go out on a limb and say you really LIKE this song. The last reason is that this song is easy to play. Very easy.

Before you jump into the music/tab, you need to know that "House of the Rising Sun" is in the Key of A minor. That means that the A scale is slightly different from a regular A scale. In the A minor scale, the C# notes become Cs, and are played on the A string at the third fret. Instead of playing a G#, in the key of A minor, we'll play just plain old G, which is the E string at the third fret. Practice this scale below.

63

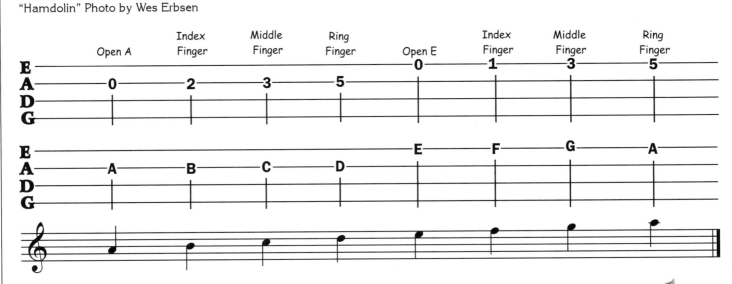

ICE COLD LICKS: You'll find "House of the Rising Sun" easy to play because the entire song is built on one little rhythmic phrase of a quarter note followed by a half note. You'll see this all through the song, beginning with the first note.

64

WARM LICKS: On some or all of the half notes you can play the Half Note Rhythm #1 (see page 75).

65

House of the Rising Sun

Tempo: Slow Sleaze

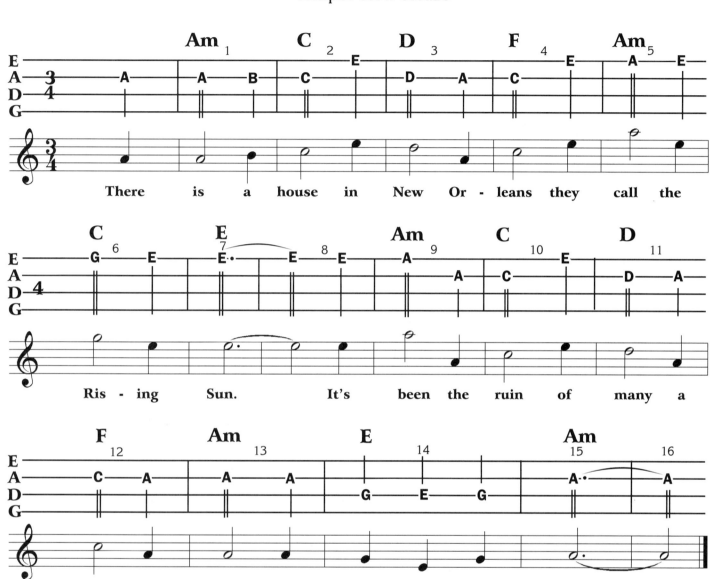

There is a house in New Or - leans they call the

Ris - ing Sun. It's been the ruin of many a

girl, and me, oh Lord, I'm one.

My mother was a tailor,
She sewed them new blue jeans,
My father was a gamblin' man,
Way down in New Orleans.

The only thing a gambler needs,
Is a suitcase and a trunk,
And the only time he's satisfied
Is when he's on a drunk.

Go and tell my baby sister
Not to do what I have done
But to shun that house in New Orleans
They call the Rising Sun.

I've Just Seen the Rock of Ages

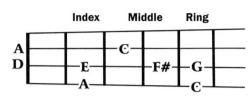

This fairly recent composition has become a bluegrass gospel classic as recorded by Ralph Stanley and Larry Sparks. Not much is known about John B. Preston, the composer of the words and

Photo by Walker Evans

music of "I've Just Seen the Rock of Ages," other than he was from Kentucky and spent some time in prison.

ICE COLD LICKS: This song is not in the normal A scale, but instead uses some minor notes that give it that lonesome flavor. Notice that instead of the customary C#, you'll play a C and where you would normally play a G#, here you play a G. Be sure to use your ring finger on all the notes on the fifth fret and your index for everything on the second fret. For the other notes, use your middle finger.

WARM LICKS: The only appropriate rhythm for this slow and emotional song is the Tremolo. Remember to use the FINGERS of your picking hand, not your arm, to get the fastest Tremolo. On the last three notes of measures 3 and 7, go DOWN UP DOWN with your pick.

Harmony Notes

When the melody is on the A string, play the E string open for harmony. On the melody notes found on the D string, you can play the G string open for the harmony. At the end of the second and fourth lines, the melody will dip down to the low A note, which is played on the G string at the second fret. When playing this note, you can also play the D string at the second fret, which will give you an E, which is part of the A chord. For those of you with jumbo fingers, you can mash your index finger down on BOTH the G and D strings at the second fret, which will give you an A and an E note. If you have tiny little fingers, you can use your index and middle fingers to do the job.

I've Just Seen the Rock of Ages

Tempo: Slow and Mournful

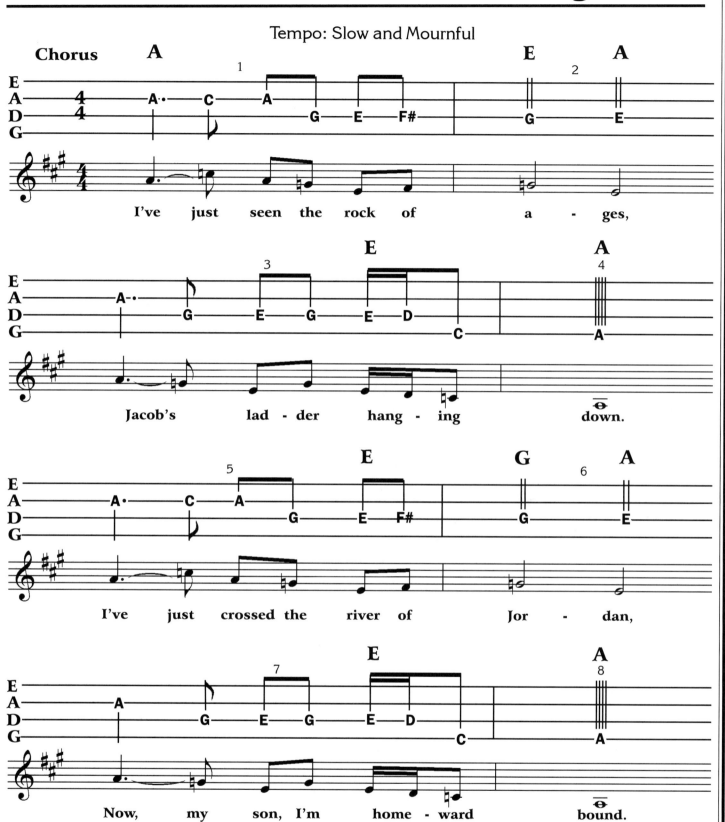

I was standing by the bedside,
Where my feeble mother lay,
When she called me close beside her
And I thought I heard her say.

As we gathered all around her,
The tears begin to fill our eyes.
Then she called me close beside her
Whispered softly her good-bye. (Chorus)

Paul and Silas

As early as the year 1800, large numbers of people traveled on wagon, horseback and on foot to attend religious camp meetings that were held in the Kentucky wilderness. These gatherings often took place on the banks of a river and sometimes lasted up to a week. In addition to the preaching and praying, there was, of course, singing. Because people came from all different churches, denominations and races, hymnbooks were rare. Even for those who knew how to read, it would have been hard to follow these songbooks during evening services which were often lit by pine knot torches. Instead of relying on the printed page, songleaders simplified hymns by creating a chorus that was so simple that virtually anyone could sing along with it.

	Index		Middle		Ring
A		B		C#	
		E		F#	G#

"Paul and Silas" is a song that strongly reflects the influence of these camp meeting spirituals, as they were called. It was first recorded on January 29, 1932, by "Snowball & Sunshine." The first bluegrass version was by Red Allen, who recorded it on the Kentucky label in late 1953 or early 1954. It was later recorded by the Stanley Brothers, Carl Story, Flatt & Scruggs, and the Country Gentlemen, among others.

ICE COLD LICKS: In addition to being easy to sing, "Paul and Silas" is easy to play because it contains a lot of repetition. You'll notice  that lines one and three are identical and that line two copies the phrasing of these lines.

WARM LICKS: Use the Watermelon lick on any or all of the quarter notes.

HOT LICKS: In measures 1 and 9 the E quarter note is followed by an E eighth note. You can easily modify your Watermelon lick to combine the E eighth note with the quarter note. Merely hold down the E note and go "Wa-ter-mel-on-rind," or DOWN-UP, DOWN-UP, DOWN with your pick. You can also use the Watermelon Rind lick on the dotted quarter notes in measures 3, 7 and 11.

Harmony Notes

All the melody notes of "Paul and Silas" are on the D or A strings. To play the harmony of any melody note on the D note, simply play the A string open. For melody notes on the A string, you'll find the harmony by playing the E string open.

Key of A

Paul and Silas

Tempo: Medium Bouncy

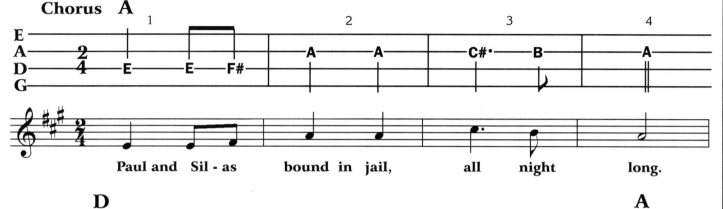

Chorus A

Paul and Sil - as   bound in jail,   all   night   long.

D   A

Paul and Sil - as   bound in jail,   all   night   long.

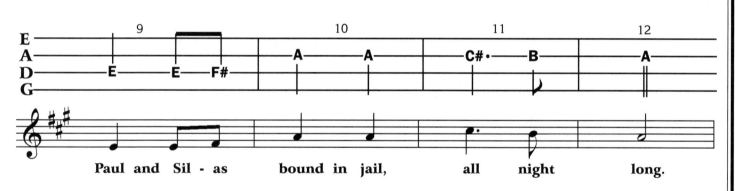

Paul and Sil - as   bound in jail,   all   night   long.

E   A

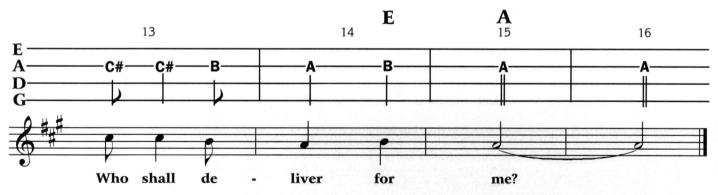

Who shall de - liver   for   me?

Paul and Silas prayed to God,
All, night long,
Paul and Silas prayed to God,
All, night long,
Paul and Silas prayed to God,
All, night long,
Who shall deliver for me?

That old jailer locked the door,
All night long,
That old jailer locked the door,
All night long,
That old jailer locked the door,
All night long,
Who shall deliver for me?

Key of F

The key of F suffers from a bad rap. In fact, most musicians FEAR playing in the key of F. Maybe it's because F is the chord most guitar players struggle with, and they just think anything with the letter "F" should be avoided at all costs. Well, fear no more! The key of F is easy on the mandolin, and in many ways, is the PERFECT mandolin key. Stay with me here.

	Index		Middle		Ring	
A	B♭			C		
		E	F			G

Photo by Wayne Erbsen

Here is the F scale. For starters, begin with the F in the middle of the staff and work your way up the scale (to the right). Then play around with the entire scale. Be sure to use your middle finger on the third fret, your index finger on the first and second fret and your ring finger on the fifth fret.

Photo by Martin Fox

71

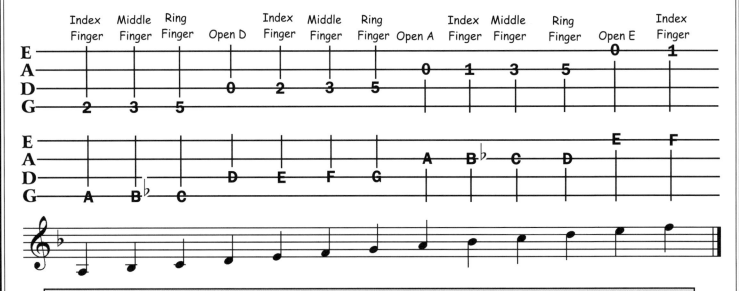

Harmony Notes

Finding the harmony of "Banks of the Ohio" is easy if you remember that any note in a chord is in harmony with every other note in that chord. As you are picking out the melody, keep in mind that the harmony has to be on an adjacent string to the melody, and is one of the notes of the chord you are on.

Banks of the Ohio

Tempo: Second Gear

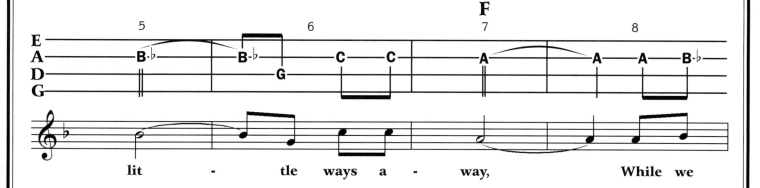

I asked my love to take a walk, just a

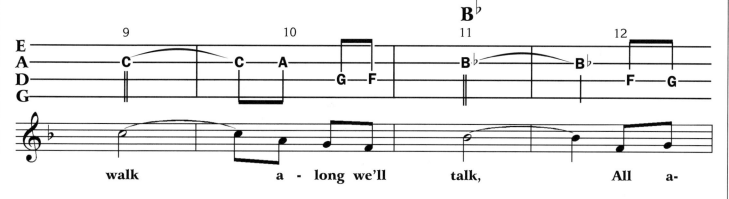

lit - tle ways a - way, While we

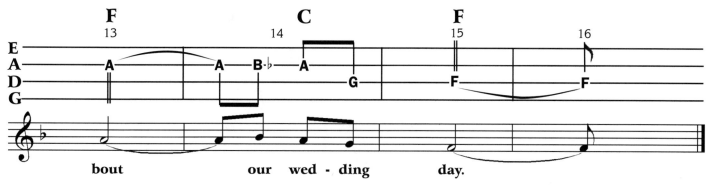

walk a - long we'll talk, All a-

bout our wed - ding day.

ICE COLD LICKS: You'll find the melody of "Banks of the Ohio" unusually easy to play.

72

WARM LICKS: This is a great tune for your Watermelon or Gallop on the half notes (with two vertical lines). Play either of these rhythms once for each quarter note and twice for each half note.

73

Bury Me Beneath the Willow

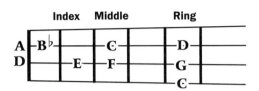

Based on how often it shows up in folk song collections and recordings, "Bury Me Beneath the Willow" certainly ranks as one of the most popular traditional songs. Starting with Henry Whitter's December 10, 1923, recording, a short list of artists who have recorded it include Ernest Thompson, George Reneau, Kelly Harrell, Ernest V. Stoneman, Dick Burnett & Leonard Rutherford, Lester McFarland & Robert A. Gardner (Mac and Bob), the Monroe Brothers and the Delmore Brothers. On August 1, 1927, the Carter Family chose it as the first song that they ever recorded. Despite my efforts to uncover the origins of "Bury Me Beneath the Willow," its author still remains a mystery.

ICE COLD LICKS: There's nothing tricky about picking out "Bury Me Beneath the Willow," so go to town!

WARM LICKS: Use the good ole Tremolo to suck all the emotional juices out of this tear-filled song.

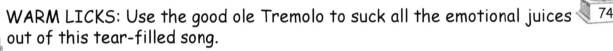

Photo by Wayne Erbsen

Harmony Notes

Just like "Banks of the Ohio," you'll find the harmony of "Bury Me Beneath the Willow" on the next string over from the melody, and the note will be part of the chord you are on.

Key of F — Bury Me Beneath the Willow

Tempo: Medium Pokey

My heart is sad and I am lonely,
For the only one I love,
When shall I see her, oh, no never,
'Til we meet in heaven above. (Chorus)

She told me that she dearly loved me,
How could I believe it untrue.
Until the angels softly whispered,
She will prove untrue to you. (Chorus)

Knoxville Girl

T his grisly murder ballad is one of a number of ballads, such as "Banks of the Ohio," in which a pregnant girlfriend is killed by her jealous lover on the banks of a river. But unlike these songs that were penned by American songwriters, "Knoxville Girl" originated in England. American versions include "The Oxford Girl," "The Wexford Girl" and "The Lexington Girl." First to record "Knoxville Girl" was Riley Puckett on March 7, 1924.

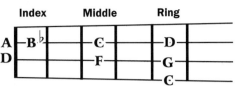

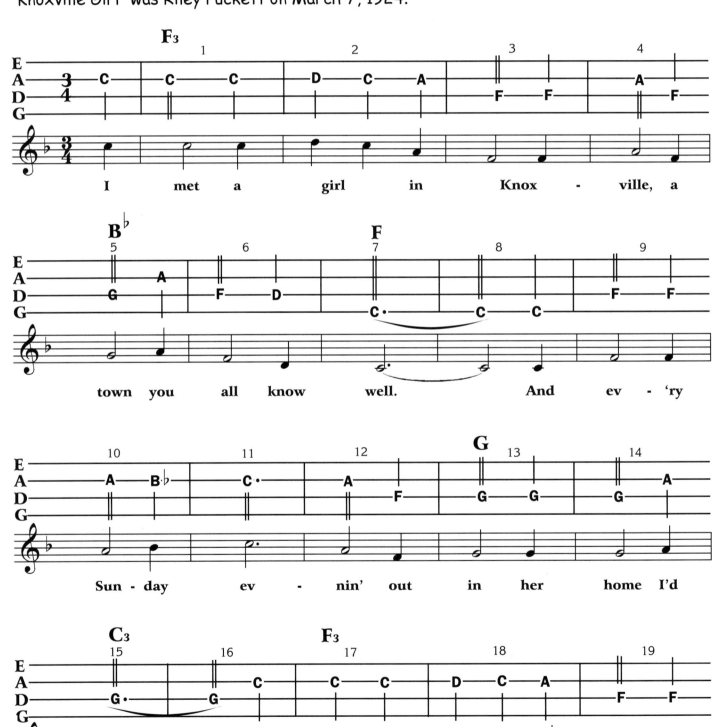

Knoxville Girl

Tempo: Bouncy Waltz

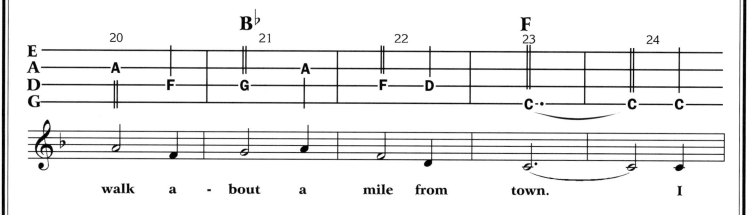

walk a - bout a mile from town. I

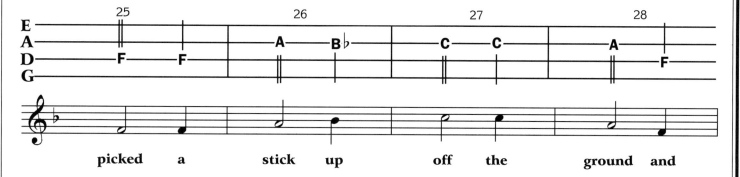

picked a stick up off the ground and

knocked that fair girl down.

ICE COLD LICKS: This pretty melody belies the tragedy of this murder ballad.

WARM LICKS: Try the Tremolo on any, some, or all of the half notes.

HOT LICKS; In "Knoxville Girl," which is in 3/4 or waltz time, you can use the Gallop to replace any half note. In measure one, for example, you would go DOWN DOWN-UP on the first C, then another down for the second C. In measure three, you can do the same thing you did in measure one (DOWN DOWN-UP DOWN).

59

The Key of C

Some mandolin pickers make a face when asked to play in the key of C, but actually it's one of my favorite keys to play in. Why? Because it's almost the same as playing in the key of G, except moved over one string. Let me show you. Play the G scale starting with the G note on the D string. Now do it again, using the same fingerings, but start on the low C note with your ring finger. Done? You just played a low C scale.

The C Scale
C, D, E, F, G, A, B, C

79

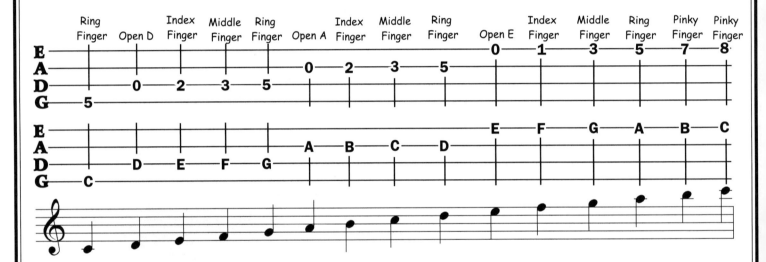

THE COLD HARD TRUTH: I'm not going to pull the wool over your eyes and tell you that "Dig a Hole in the Meadow" is one of those push-over easy songs that you can play with one hand tied behind your back standing on one foot. It's not. What we have here is a wonderfully bluesy melody that you should save to play until you have many of the other tunes in this book under your belt. You'll then be ready to navigate the twists and turns of this squirrely but fun melody.

THE BLUES SCALE: After you hitch up your belt and roll up your sleeves, mess around and get familiar with the blues scale shown in the chart to the right. You'll see some strange notes in there. These notes are not really hard, they're just notes we seldom use. We'll use these same notes in "Dig a Hole in the Meadow."

	Index	Middle		Ring	Pinky
E					
A	Bb	C			D#
	D#	E	F	G	
				C	

LISTEN: Wear out the CD that comes with this book so that you're totally familiar with this tune. Try singing the words along with the notes you hear on the CD. Pay particular attention to which fingers of your left hand to use by double checking with the chart above. Once you get this tune down, you'll find it so addicting that your family will have to hit you with a stick to make you stop playing it.

80

Dig a Hole in the Meadow

Tempo: Very Bouncy

Dig a hole, dig a hole in the mead - ow, Dig a hole in the cold, cold ground. Dig a hole, in the mead - ow, gon - na lay darlin' Co - ry down.

Go away, go away Darlin' Cory,
And bring to me my gun.
I ain't no man for trouble,
But I'll die before I run.

Wake up, wake up darlin' Cory,
Go and do the best you can.
I've got me another woman,
You can hunt you another man.

61

I've Been All Around This World

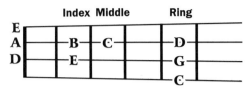

This is what we call a "true song," because it's about something that actually happened. In this case, the outlaw immortalized in this song was hanged for murder in Fort Smith, Arkansas, in the 1870s. Chances are good that he was sentenced to die by the famous hanging judge, the Honorable Isaac Charles Parker, who sentenced one hundred and sixty men to the gallows. Adjusting the noose was Parker's chief executioner, George Maledon, who took pride in his "scientific hangings." Oh boy!

ICE COLD LICKS: The basic melody should be a snap to play once you listen to the CD and get familiar with the song.

WARM LICKS: After you get comfortable playing the basic melody, try adding the Hot Dog to either or both notes of any pair of the eighth notes.

HOT LICKS: On the quarter note of your choice, you can play the Gallop or the Porcupine.

The Stanley Brothers

Harmony Notes

When the melody's on the D string, you can play the G string along with it. On the note where the melody dips down to the G string, your harmony is the D string at the second fret.

I've Been All Around This World

Tempo: Medium Heat

Key of C

Working on the new railroad with mud up to my knees,
Working on the new railroad with mud up to my knees,
Working for big John Henry and he's so hard to please,
I've been all around this world.

Wildwood Flower

Index Middle   Ring

```
E ──────────────────────
A ────────── C ────── D ─
D ────── E ── F ────── G ─
                      C ─
```

I like to think of "Wildwood Flower" as "the hill-billy national anthem" because it is the tune every country guitar player wants to play. Since guitar pickers often play it in the key of C, that's where we'll play it so they won't have to play it by themselves. Originally titled "I'll Twine Mid the Ringlets," the Carter Family called it "Wildwood Flower" on their May 5, 1928, recording for Victor. The words were composed in 1860 by J.P. Webster and the melody by Maud Irving. By the way, Webster also composed the Civil War classic, "Lorena."

ICE COLD LICKS: This classic melody doesn't need much decorating because it's fine just the way it is.

84   WARM LICKS: If you like, you can add the Hot Dog to any of the eighth notes.

85

HOT LICKS: The quarter notes are a perfect place to play either the Watermelon, the Gallop or the Porcupine. Better yet, mix them up!

86

The Carter Family

Harmony Notes

When the melody's on the D string, play the G string as a harmony and when the melody's on the A string, use the E string for harmony. In measures 4, 9 and 18 you'll notice the melody is the C note played at the fifth fret of the G string. For harmony, you can use the D string at the second fret.

Wildwood Flower

Tempo: A Comfortable Trot

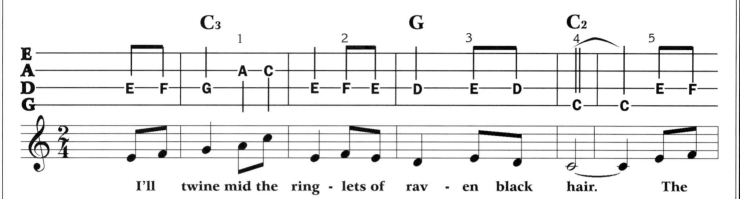

I'll twine mid the ring - lets of rav - en black hair. The

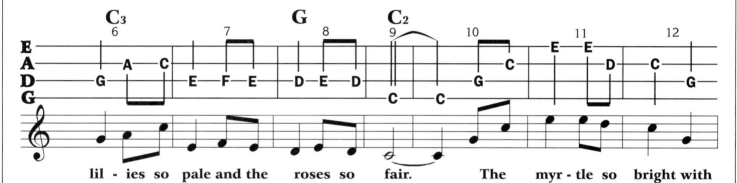

lil - ies so pale and the roses so fair. The myr - tle so bright with

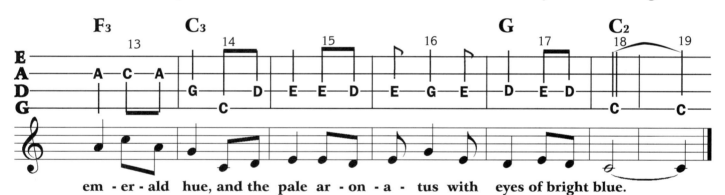

em - er - ald hue, and the pale ar - on - a - tus with eyes of bright blue.

I'll sing and I'll dance my laugh shall be gay
I'll cease this wild weeping, drive sorrow away;
Tho' my heart is now breaking he never shall know
That his name made me tremble and my pale cheek to glow.

I'll think of him never, I'll be wildly gay,
I'll charm every heart and the crowd I will sway;
I'll live yet to see him regret the dark hour
When he won then neglected the frail wildwood flower.

He told me he loved me, and promised to love
Through ill and misfortune, all other above;
Another has won him, oh! misery to tell
He left me in silence, no words of farewell!

The Key of D

You'll soon discover that the fingering on your new D scale is the same as it was on the A scale. But instead of starting the scale on the A string, we'll begin with the D string open. Notice that the location of the notes is the same on both the A and the D strings.

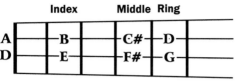

D Scale:
D, E, F#, G, A, B, C#, D

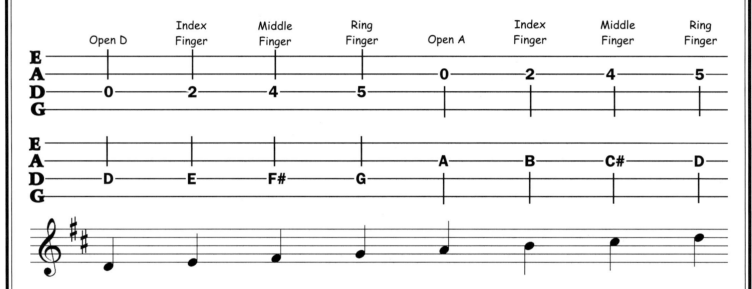

Dock Walsh

"In the Pines" is a favorite old folk song, turned bluegrass song, that originated around the time of the Civil War. It was first recorded by Dock Walsh in Atlanta, Georgia, on April 17, 1926. To add spice to this story, Ill mention that Walsh traveled on foot, uninvited, from his home in Wilkes county, North Carolina, to the offices of Columbia records in Atlanta, Georgia, carrying his heavy Gibson banjo. After traveling a distance of over 300 miles, it's no wonder he's sitting down in this photo! Perhaps his walking feat alone earned him a chance to record.

ICE COLD LICKS: You'll find this melody very simple to play. On all the eighth notes, be sure to go DOWN-UP with your pick.

WARM LICKS: On any of the half notes, you can play the Tremolo (page 73) or the Watermelon (page 74).

Key of D

In the Pines

Tempo: Pitifully Slow

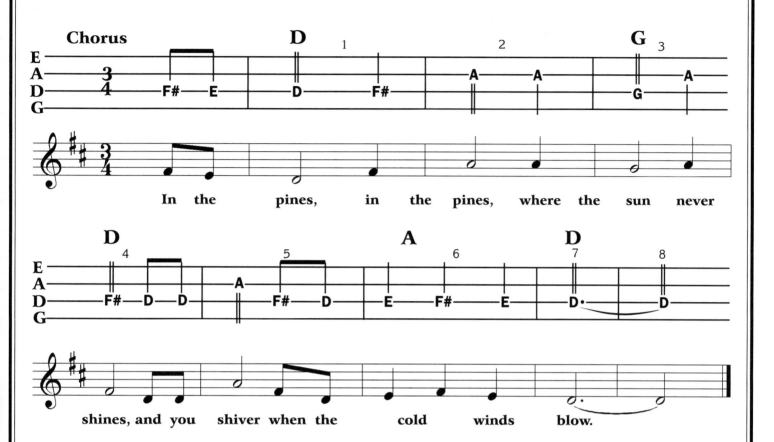

In the pines, in the pines, where the sun never shines, and you shiver when the cold winds blow.

The longest train I ever saw,
Went down that Georgia line.
The engine passed at six o'clock
And the cab went by at nine. (Chorus)

Little girl, little girl, don't lie to me,
Tell me, where'd you stay last night?
I stayed in the pines where the sun never shines
And I shivered when the cold winds blow. (Chorus)

I asked my captain for the time of day,
He said he threwed his watch away.
It's a long steel rail and a short crosstie,
I'm on my way back home. (Chorus)

Charlie and Bill Monroe

Harmony Notes

When the melody is a D, an E or an F# on the D string, play the A string open as harmony. In measure 2, play the D string open to harmonize with the A string open. When the melody goes to a G on the D string in measure 3, play the G string open.

Midnight on the Stormy Deep

Despite the presence of a sizable population of German settlers in the southern mountains during early frontier days, it was clearly the Scots Irish immigrants who contributed most to what would be called Appalachian or old-time music. "Midnight on the Stormy Deep" is one of the few songs that can be traced directly to Germany. Folklorist Gus Meade found that Wilhelm Hauff wrote this traditional German song. Country music historian Bill C. Malone has pointed out that it was published in America before the Civil War. The first recording was on October 16, 1928, by Mac and Bob, who called it "Midnight on the Stormy Sea."

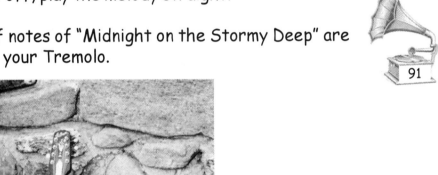

	Index	Middle	Ring
E			
A	B		D
D	E	F#	
	A		

"Midnight on the Stormy Deep" is simply a great tune to play on the mandolin. It's slow enough to give us time to play the melody without throwing a double conniption, and it's a perfect vehicle to play our Tremolo.

90 ICE COLD LICKS: First off, play the melody straight.

TOASTY WARM LICKS: The half notes of "Midnight on the Stormy Deep" are the perfect platform for playing your Tremolo.

91

Photo by Wayne Erbsen

Harmony Notes
When the melody's on the D string, play the A string as a harmony, and when the melody's on the A string, use the D string for harmony.

Key of D Midnight on the Stormy Deep

Tempo: Rather Pokey

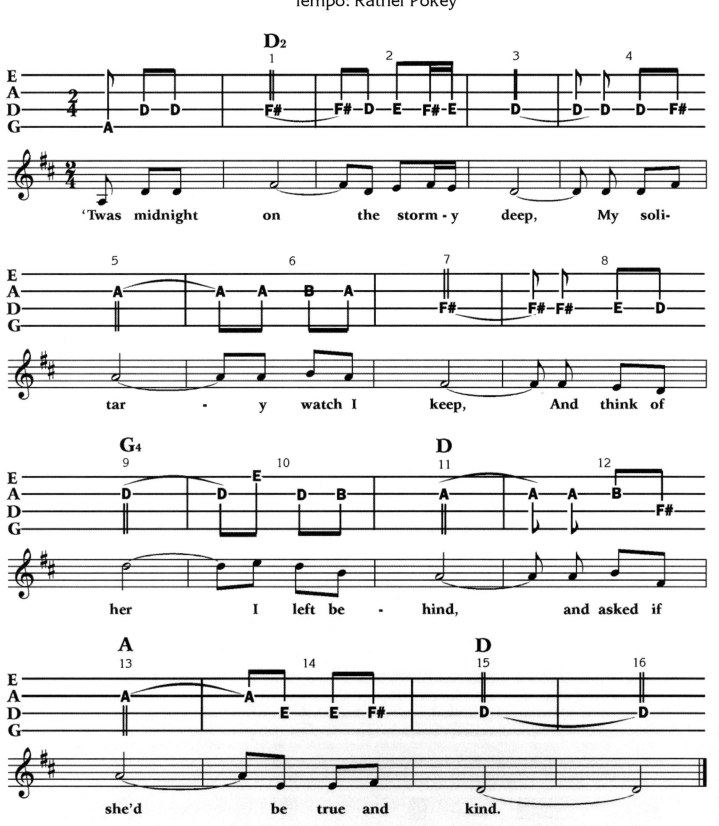

'Twas midnight on the storm-y deep, My soli-
tar - y watch I keep, And think of
her I left be - hind, and asked if
she'd be true and kind.

I never shall forget the day
That I was forced to go away.
In silence there my head she'd rest
And pressed me to her loving breast.

Oh, Willie, don't go back to sea
There's other girls as good as me.
But none can love you true as I
Pray don't go where the bullets fly.

Soldier's Joy

Of all the old-time fiddle tunes, "Soldier's Joy" is certainly the granddaddy of them all. It may not be the oldest tune, but over the years it has proven itself to be the most popular and widely circulated of any fiddle tune you can name. It apparently originated in England under the title "The King's Head." One legend tells that a condemned man played it for the king and was apparently spared. Besides "Soldier's Joy," American fiddler's have called it "Payday in the Army," and "Love Somebody." First to record it were Samantha Bumgarner and Eva Davis, who traveled from western North Carolina to New York City in November of 1924. They made their mark on country music history when they sat and played their fiddle and banjo into an acoustical horn. This was back in the dawn of recording technology, when microphones were only a gleam in a recording engineer's eyes.

"Soldiers Joy" will be a good tune for you to learn. It's so well known that you can be confident that virtually any experienced old-time or bluegrass player will know it. It's a notey little tune, so you'll need to have your D scale down solid.

STONE COLD LICKS: The sobering news is that there IS no ice cold way to play the melody of "Soldier's Joy" because there are a lot of melody notes to play. Remember when you see the eighth notes to use a DOWN stroke on the first eighth note, and an UP stroke on the second eighth note.

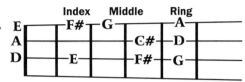

Photo by Wayne Erbsen

Soldier's Joy

Tempo: Pretty Peppy

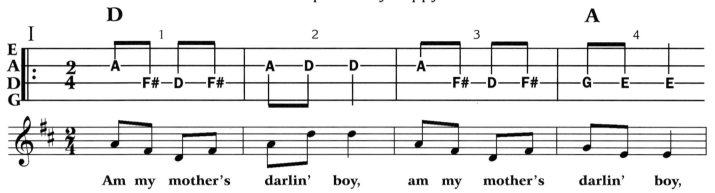

Am my mother's darlin' boy, am my mother's darlin' boy,

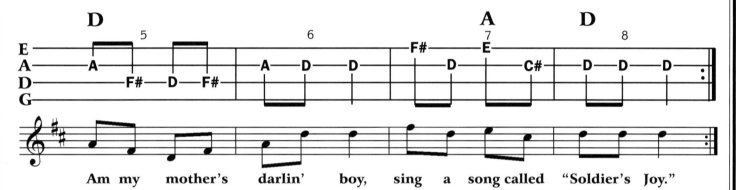

Am my mother's darlin' boy, sing a song called "Soldier's Joy."

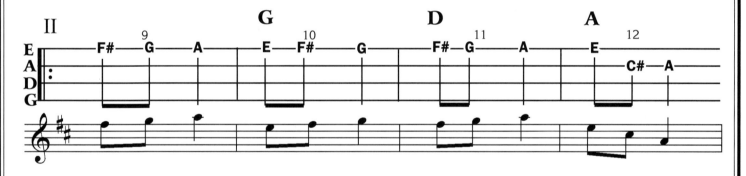

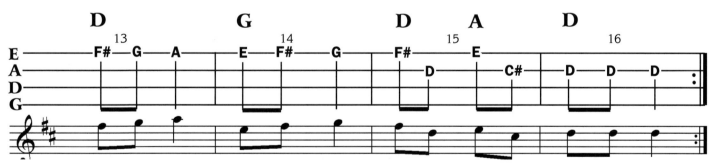

Chicken in the bread pan scratching out dough
Granny will your dog bite? No, child, no!
Ladies to the center and gents catch air
Hold her, Newt, don't let her rare!

Twenty-five cents for the morphine
Fifteen cents for the beer
Twenty-five cents for the morphine
They're gonna take me away from here.

71

How to Jam

Playing unaccompanied mandolin is a joy not to be sneezed at, but even better is jamming with other pickers and singers. If you're like most beginners, you can't imagine the day when you'll be good enough to actually play music with other humans. The fact is, you may be ready right now. The worst case scenario is that you might have to read this page first, and then you'll be set to play with other folks.

Playing music with other musicians generally means using just two skills: 1) chopping chords while keeping the rhythm and 2) playing the melody or the lead. On page 15 we talked about how to play the chop and on page 78 is a page of simple chords to play while chopping the rhythm. When the day comes and you work up your nerve to saunter up to an ongoing jam session, sidle up to a friendly looking person and whisper these words out of the corner of your mouth: "Say, what key is this song in?" They'll probably say G or A, but you never know what might come out of their mouth (especially if they're chewing tobacco!) Then sneak off to a quiet corner and secretly open to page 72 of this book. In the first vertical column of this chart, you'll find all the keys you're likely to find in a bluegrass jam. What you need to know is that for any key, most bluegrass songs will only use three chords. These chords have been given Roman numerals by some wise person: I, IV and V. So for the key of G, for example, the I chord will be G, the IV chord is C and the V chord is D.

Key	Ⓘ	II	Ⓘ Ⓥ	Ⓥ	VI
A	A	B	D	E	F#m
B	B	C#	E	F#	G#m
C	C	D	F	G	Am
D	D	E	G	A	Bm
E	E	F#	A	B	C#m
F	F	G	B♭	C	Dm
G	G	A	C	D	Em

When approaching a jam session, always position yourself so you are facing the most intelligent looking guitar player in the group. With one eye, keep a bead on their left, or chording hand. Learn what a G, a C and a D look like on the guitar. When they change chords, you change chords. With your other eye, watch their right hand. If they know what they're doing, their right hand will play one of the low strings on their guitar, and then they'll strum down on the higher strings. With any luck, their rhythm will be One-TWO, with the accent on the TWO. The Two is when you chop your chord. If the guitar player is impossible to follow, then tap your foot to the music while saying "One-TWO" Chop only on the TWO. How do you know what chords to play if there's no guitar to follow? The verse of most bluegrass songs will generally start and end on the I chord. It'll change to the IV or V chord in the middle, but then it will often come back to the I chord. Remember to keep good rhythm with your chop, even if your chording fingers are hopelessly confused. With a little determination and persistence, you'll soon be a jammer.

Mandolin Rhythms in 2/4 or 4/4 Time

1. THE TREMOLO is the most "mandoliny" of all the rhythms we can play on the instrument. To play the Tremolo, your pick will rapidly go DOWN-UP over and over. Most of the motion should be in the fingers, not the arm. Be sure to keep your wrist loose. Think of the Tremolo as a throttle that can affect the emotion of a song just by speeding it up, or slowing it down. Your goal should be to have a fast Tremolo so you can really make a song drip with emotion.

2. THE HOT DOG. This dandy little rhythm is a way of playing two notes which sounds like "hot dog." Play the "hot" with a DOWN stroke of your pick and the "dog" with an UP stroke. Try it on any note of your mandolin, while saying "hot dog, hot dog" as you pick it. (Make sure no one hears you saying this.) Each Hot Dog is the same as two sixteenth notes. Whenever you see a song in the book with two eighth notes, you can substitute a Hot Dog for each of the eighth notes. For example, look at "Shady Grove" on

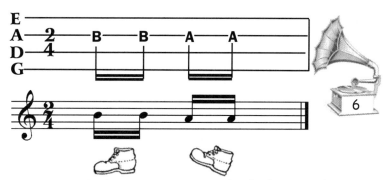

page 43. The first two notes in measure one are eighth notes. Instead of playing those eighth notes as written, substitute a Hot Dog for each of the notes. In music lingo, you're merely playing four sixteenth notes instead of two eighth notes.

3. THE GALLOP has the rhythm of the word "do-hickey," and takes up one beat. The timing is long, short-short. Your pick will play DOWN, DOWN-UP. Your foot would go DOWN on the first note (which is the melody note), and DOWN-UP on the two quick notes.

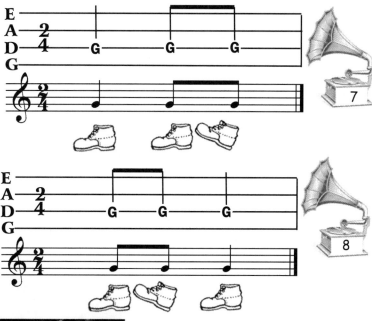

4. THE PORCUPINE sounds like the rhythm of the critter: "Porcu- pine." Go DOWN-UP-DOWN with your pick. Your foot goes DOWN-UP on the pair of eighth notes ("por-cu") and DOWN on the last note ("pine.")

Mandolin Rhythms in 2/4 or 4/4 Time

5. THE WATERMELON. Go DOWN-UP, DOWN-UP with your pick. The rhythm sounds like "wa-ter-mel-on." Your foot goes DOWN-UP-DOWN-UP. The four notes can be played evenly, but you can also accent the first of the four notes, (**wa**-ter-mel-on) or the third note (wa-ter-*mel*-on).

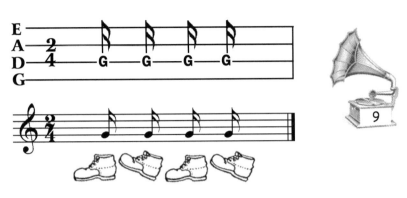

6. GOING t' TOWN. This lick sounds like "going t' town." Be sure your pick goes DOWN-UP-UP-DOWN. Your pick should hit DOWN on "go," UP and "ing," UP on "t'" and DOWN on "town." This lick takes the place of a half note, or two quarter notes.

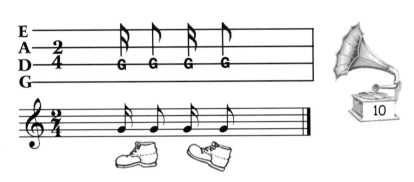

7. ECHO NOTES: Instead of playing any quarter note, you can choose to play two eighth notes. We'll call the second eighth note an Echo Note because it echos the melody. Any note of a chord can be played as an echo. The chart below shows you the three notes that make up some common chords. The root, third, and fifth notes are all in harmony with each other and any of these three notes can serve as an echo of the melody. Try this out in measure one of "Little Maggie," page 34.

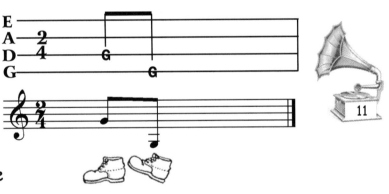

Chord	Root	Third	Fifth
A	A	C#	E
B	B	D#	F#
C	C	E	G
D	D	F#	A
E	E	G#	B
F	F	A	C
G	G	B	D

Mandolin Rhythms in Waltz or 3/4 Time

1. Basic Waltz Rhythm # 1: *ONE, TWO - THREE* or DOWN, DOWN- UP with your pick. This is your basic rhythm for accompanying songs in waltz time. You can play one, several, or all the notes of the chord.

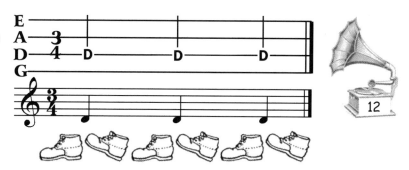

2. Basic Waltz Rhythm #2: *ONE, TWO AND THREE.* With your pick, go **DOWN**, DOWN-UP-DOWN. *A variation of Basic Waltz Rhythm #1.*

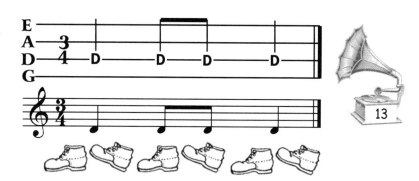

3. Basic Waltz Rhythm #3: *ONE-TWO, ONE-TWO ONE* or **DOWN-UP-DOWN-UP-DOWN** with your pick. *Yet another variation of above.*

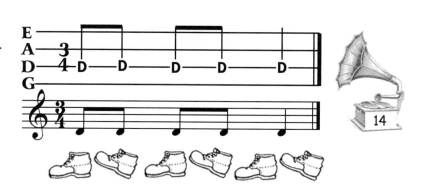

4. Half Note Rhythm #1: **ONE-TWO, ONE** or **DOWN**-UP, DOWN with your pick. Takes up one half note or two beats.

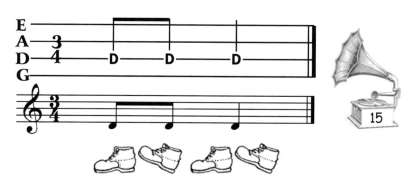

5. Half Note Rhythm #2: **ONE-TWO, ONE-TWO** or **DOWN**-UP, DOWN-UP with your pick. Takes up one half note or two beats.

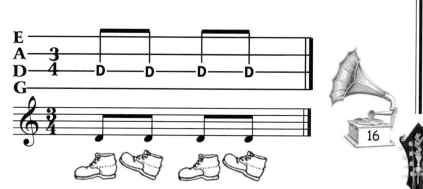

Harmony Chord Positions

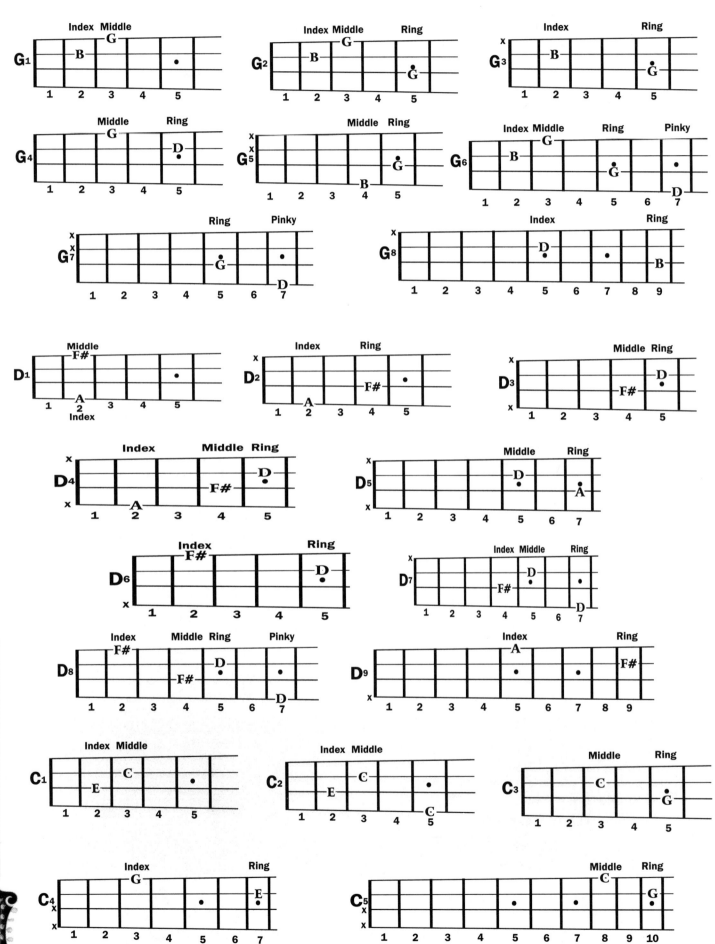

Harmony Chord Positions

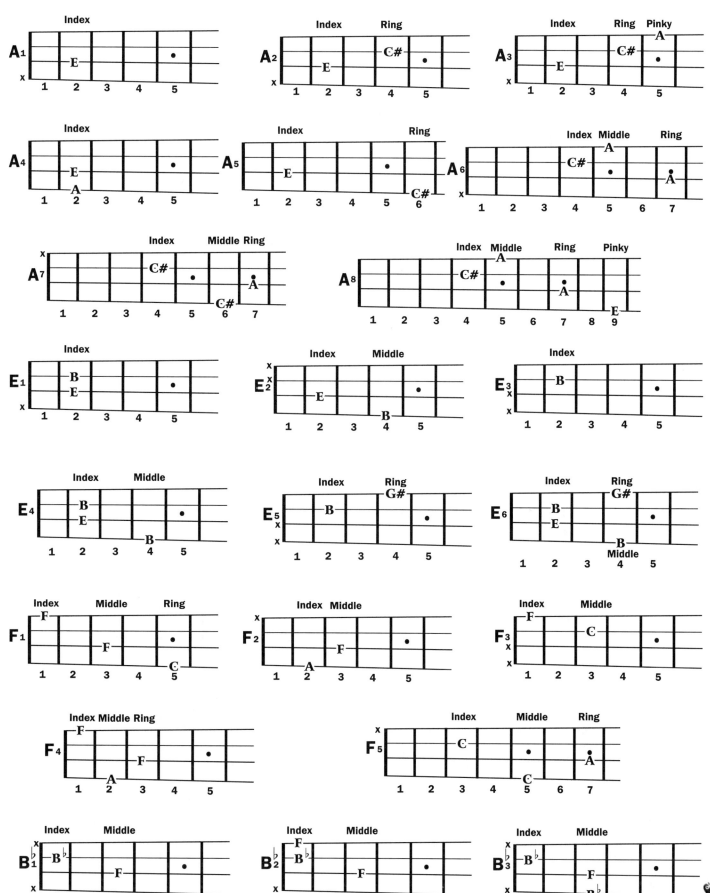

Simple Rhythm Chord Positions

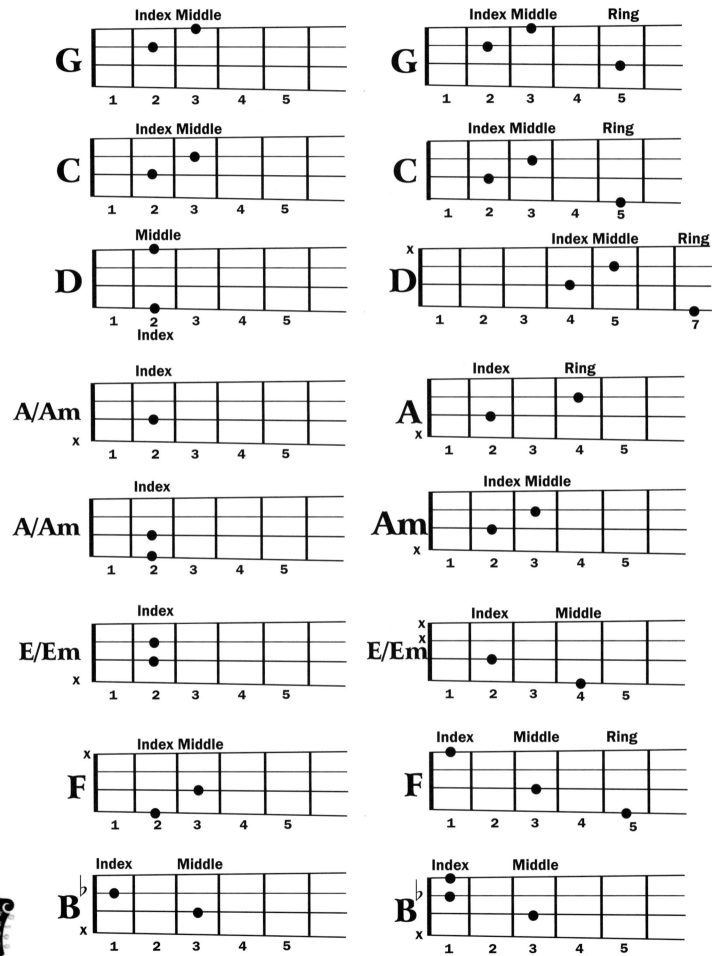

Tune & CD Index

Photo by Bucky Hanks

Wayne Erbsen

Native Ground Books & Music

Books of Music, Lore & Home Cookin'

Music Instruction

Bluegrass Banjo for the Complete Ignoramus
Companion to Bluegrass Banjo for the Complete Ignoramus
Bluegrass Jamming on Banjo
Bluegrass Jamming on Fiddle
Bluegrass Jamming on Mandolin
Clawhammer Banjo for the Complete Ignoramus
Clawhammer Banjo: Tunes, Tips & Jamming
Easy 2-Chord Songs for Guitar
Easy 2-Chord Songs for Mandolin
Flatpicking Guitar for the Complete Ignoramus
Painless Guitar
Old-Time Fiddle for the Complete Ignoramus
Ukulele for the Complete Ignoramus

Home Cookin'

1st American Cookie Lady
A Garden Supper Tonight
Aunt Barb's Bread Book
Children at the Hearth
Early American Cookery
Log Cabin Cooking
Lost Art of Pie Making
Mama's in the Kitchen
Old-Time Farmhouse Cooking
Picnic Time
Pioneer Village Cookbook
Secrets of the Great Old-Timey Cooks
Take Two & Butter 'Em While They're Hot!

Songs & Lore

Backpocket Bluegrass Songbook
Cowboy Songs, Jokes, Lingo n' Lore
Front Porch Songs, Jokes & Stories
Hymns of the Old Camp Ground
Log Cabin Pioneers
Manners & Morals of Victorian America
The Outhouse Papers
Railroad Fever
Rousing Songs of the Civil War
Rural Rotos of Bluegrass
Singing Rails

Write or call for a FREE catalog
Native Ground Books & Music
109 Bell Road
Asheville, NC 28805 (800) 752-2656
info@nativeground.com
www.nativeground.com